OneGenAway is doing the work, not just talking about it. I've watched Pastor Chris Whitney lead this organization from its inception and I heartily endorse the story, the people, and the results.

David Yoder
Pastor, Faith Community Church

The name OneGenAway is a revolutionary term within itself. We understand it suggests that hunger, racial prejudice, and denominational separation can be removed in one generation. In our society we know this is a God-sized task. However, this ministry has made a tremendous physical impact in our community in the number of people fed, the number of meetings across denominational lines, and the number of multiracial group gatherings. *The Dirty Church* explains that OneGenAway has provided an opportunity for everyday people to practice Jesus' teachings on giving, witnessing, and having no respecter of person. Thanks OneGenAway for both your physical and spiritual impact on all of us!

Hewitt C. Sawyers
Pastor, West Harpeth Primitive Baptist Church

OneGenAway is a perfect opportunity for our students to develop empathy for the needs of others in their own community. Once they know of these needs, students will have an innate desire to serve, which in turn can have a transformational impact on how they see themselves and others around them. Our students have asked over and over if they can continue to help, whether it is boxing up food or helping with the food distributions. We look forward to strengthening our relationship with OneGenAway over the next few years.

Brian Bass, Ed. D.
Principal, Renaissance High

The biblical definition of *servant* and its related word *deacon* comes from the Greek word *diakanos*. The literal definition of servant/deacon is "through the dust." How appropriate! Chris and Elaine Whitney are two unique, anointed servants of God. The only way one can be a part of *The Dirty Church* is to know what it means to work "through the dust." Throughout all Scripture, Jehovah had concern for the hungry, poor, and mistreated. Jesus lets us know, "The poor you have with you always."
(John 12:8)

In the final recorded sermon of Jesus, He gives the ministry that OneGenAway is doing utmost priority.

"I was hungry and you gave me something to eat. I was thirsty and you gave me something to drink. I was a stranger and you took me in. I needed clothes and you clothed me. I was sick and you looked after me. I was in prison and you came to visit."
(Matthew 25:35-36)

We need the poor in ways beyond what they need from us. We are privileged to share material goods. Jesus translates that into heavenly treasure. We serve Him. He said, "When you serve the least of these brothers of mine, you did it for me."
(Matthew 25:40)
Dr. Albert Lemmons

OneGenAway exemplifies Christian principles in Ephesians 2:10: "We are His workmanship, created in Christ Jesus for good works, which God prepared beforehand, that we should walk in them" through service to those in need. *The Dirty Church* is a testimony of God's omnipresence to transcend and impact lives through outreach by striving to strengthen the Kingdom of God. Chris Whitney and the OneGenAway ministry have transformed the lives of many people. *The Dirty Church* provides encouragement and motivation that inspire you to give back to others.
Elder Vernon Ray McGuire, Jr.
Pastor, Green Street Church of God
Franklin, Tennessee

The very first food distribution my church participated in with OneGenAway and Pastor Chris was on the Saturday of the great Nashville flood of 2010. Since that time I have watched OneGenAway flourish and touch thousands of lives. Partnering with OneGenAway has had a tremendously positive effect on our church. Furthermore, Pastor Chris has become a very close personal friend. His love for Jesus, passion for the poor, and commitment to wipe out hunger are unparalleled.

Rev. Kevin Riggs, PhD
Senior Pastor of Franklin Community Church
Author of "Failing Like Jesus" and "Evangelism for the 21st Century"

Chris, the love of my life,

Words cannot express how happy and excited I am for you. Finally the world gets to experience in reading these words what I have been experiencing in my heart for 29 years: your passion for people and serving others. I just love your selfless heart!

I know that our road called life has not always been the easiest route that God had us go down; but what an adventure and I would not change a thing. With all that we have been through in our marriage, though hard at times, we have always stuck together and looked to God as our compass; and through all the mountaintops and valleys, it has made us who we are today.

You have been such a godly example for me, our children, our sons-in-law, and our grandchildren—what a great heritage they get to experience because of your obedience.

We have lived by the scripture Hebrews 10:35: "Therefore, do not throw away your confidence, which has great reward. For you have need of endurance, so that after you have done the will of God, you may receive the promise."

This is your promise...and it's just the beginning. Okay, honey, I'm strapped in and ready to continue on our journey!

I love you more than you could ever imagine,

Elaine

THE DIRTY
CHURCH

THE DIRTY CHURCH

Teaching People to Love One Another
Through Service

BY
CHRIS WHITNEY

LUCIDBOOKS

FOREWORD

Before the time of Jesus, followers of a Rabbi, his Talmid, would follow the Rabbi closely. Each day, in each encounter and conversation the Rabbi would have, they would hang on his every word of wisdom. It's said that sometimes they would walk so closely with him that the dust the Rabbi's shoes would kick up on the dirty roads they walked together would begin to cover them completely.

For almost 30 years my great friend Chris Whitney has followed his rabbi, Jesus, and is covered in the dust of that Rabbi. When he contacted me recently and asked me to write the foreword for this book, *The Dirty Church*, I was honored to say yes.

I was also pleased when he told me that he was finally going to write a book about the idea God gave him, "One Generation Away." *The Dirty Church* perfectly reflects the heart of my friend and of this ministry.

It's said that from nothing God will make something. With "One Generation Away" God dropped an idea into Chris's heart years ago and Chris trusted that God would bring that idea to pass. With time, prayer, and lots of hard work by lots of people, He has.

What an amazing job Chris, his wife, Elaine, and the "One Generation Away" team have done in helping those who are fighting a hard battle. It is inspiring to see how God is using this ministry to feed so many people, help move us toward racial reconciliation, and truly demonstrate to a hurting world the love and grace of this magnificent savior we call Jesus.

In the chapters that follow, Chris shares his vison of what the "dirty" church looks like and some very practical ways we can get this dirt all over us.

Thomas Merton wrote years ago, "Do not look for pleasure, but turn away from things that satisfy your senses and your mind and look for God in hunger and thirst and darkness, through deserts of the spirit in which it seems to be madness to travel."[1]

In *The Dirty Church* Chris Whitney writes of this "madness," which the world does not understand although it craves it in its inmost being. This "madness" is Christianity itself!

I hope as you read this book you are inspired to get very dirty.

Pastor Bob Kester
St. Louis, Missouri
September 2015

---

1 Thomas Merton, *New Seeds of Contemplation* (New York: New Directions, 1961), 143-144.

ACKNOWLEDGEMENTS

I first want to acknowledge my wife, Elaine. Without her unwavering support and love, this book or One Generation Away would not have happened. Thank you for pouring your life out for our family. I am thankful for my children and their support.

Thank you to Mandy Cole for transcribing all those messages and to Mandy Miller for adding, subtracting, and helping me to make the message clear.

Thank you to Jack O'Briant, Sammantha Lengl, and The Lucid Books team for all your work.

Thank you to Scott and Rosemary Muirhead for your amazing gift to make this all possible.

Special thanks to the board at OneGenAway and all the volunteers that have made this story what it is, an act of justice and service.

CONTENTS

ONE GENERATION AWAY

In the 1930s, the United States faced the most devastating economic crisis in our nation's history: The Great Depression. Following the stock market crash in 1929, countless banks were forced to close their doors, companies to lay off their employees, and families to leave their homes. President Franklin Delano Roosevelt responded by implementing a system known as The New Deal, a series of measures which would attempt to alleviate the devastating poverty which had so swiftly ravaged the nation. In many ways, the government stepped into many of the roles that the Church is mandated to serve, and, sadly, the Church largely abdicated those responsibilities.

Fast-forward to present day. A few years ago, a group of volunteers and I were delivering commodities to a group of elderly women where I live in Franklin, Tennessee. One of these was named Ms. Rena, a 76-year-old woman who would volunteer to serve commodities. I remember one particular day when Ms. Rena was in my line to receive food. She couldn't stand for long, so she would bring her own stool to sit and wait. I've always been a hugger, and when I saw that sweet old woman that day, I decided to greet her with a hug. I remember her telling me, "Pastor, I just want to thank you so much." I said, "Oh, no,

Ms. Rena, it really is my honor to serve you." She said, "No, you don't understand. Since you're giving me food, now I can pay for my medicine." I can't even begin to tell you how many times I've heard stories like that one. She was forced to choose between food or medicine—two basic essentials for her life.

The reality is that among us today, down our streets, and even next door, there are people facing decisions like Ms. Rena's. This is poverty—making life or death choices every day. You don't have to get on a plane to find people who face those decisions daily. They are here in the United States. They are in Franklin, Tennessee. They are in your hometown.

I believe that we are a single generation away from eliminating poverty in America. But if that is to happen, it's time for the Church to get dirty. We've been way too sterile and clean. We have to embrace those mandates from the Bible to care for the poor, the widow, and the orphan. The Church has to recapture those responsibilities which for too long have been ignored. Christians sit back and critique how the government deals with issues of poverty and unemployment; meanwhile, the Word of God compels us: "If anyone has material possessions and sees a brother or sister in need but has no pity on them, how can the love of God be in that person?" (1 John 3:17 NIV). I believe that, if we would heed the call, this could be the finest hour that the Church has ever seen. I recognize the darkness and pain that exist in our culture. In first-century Corinth and Rome, the culture was hostile toward Christianity and filled with immorality of all kinds, yet the Church thrived. So instead of becoming paralyzed by the problems, it is time to stand in the promise, "He who is in you is greater than he who is in the world" (1 John 4:4).

There is a scripture that hangs on the wall just as you walk into the building of the church I pastor, and it is the foundation of what we believe as a church and what we do through our ministry, One Generation Away. The passage, framed in the foyer, reads,

> *Isaiah 58:6-12   Is this not the fast that I have chosen: to loose the bonds of wickedness, to undo the heavy burdens, to let the oppressed go free, and that you break every yoke? 7 Is it not to share your bread with the hungry, and that you bring to your house the poor who are cast out; when you see the naked, that you cover him, and not hide yourself from your own flesh? 8 Then your light shall break forth like the morning, your healing shall spring forth speedily, and your righteousness shall go before you; the glory of the Lord shall be your rear guard. 9 Then you shall call, and the Lord will answer; you shall cry, and He will say, "Here I am." If you take away the yoke from your midst, the pointing of the finger, and speaking wickedness, 10 if you extend your soul to the hungry and satisfy the afflicted soul, then your light shall dawn in the darkness, and your darkness shall be as the noonday. 11 The Lord will guide you continually, and satisfy your soul in drought, and strengthen your bones; you shall be like a watered garden, and like a spring of water, whose waters do not fail. 12 Those from among you shall build the old waste places; You shall raise up the foundations of many generations; And you shall be called the Repairer of the Breach, The Restorer of Streets to Dwell In.*

This is our mandate. God came to restore us. He sends us out to restore the world around us. But there is no way we can accomplish these things without getting dirty. We will never build the old waste places, repair the breach, or restore the streets to dwell in, if we are not willing to insert ourselves into the brokenness of our world.

The ministry One Generation Away is not a movement I created. It is a continuation of the movement Jesus began when

He said, "The Son of Man did not come to be served, but to serve." One day I was at Starbucks sitting across from Pastor Hewitt Sawyers, who is now my close friend. At the time, we had just met, and he asked me, "Tell me something about your church." I told him, "Our church loves to serve other churches and other ministries." He looked at me, leaned back in his chair, and said, "In 30 years, I've never ever heard a pastor say that." A part of me wanted to pat myself on the back, but, instead, it made my heart sink. How could it be that in 30 years this man had never heard another pastor say, "I'd like to serve you"? Imagine what the world would look like if the Church embraced that. So I started to pray.

Prayer is how our ministry started. My wife and I married 29 years ago in Greenville, Mississippi. We quickly became very involved in ministry; twelve years later we felt God moving in our hearts to start a church. Long story short, we both prayed separately for a couple of days; then came back together, and I said, "I feel like we're supposed to go to Nashville." She replied, "Me too." My wife is from Greenville, and I'm from St. Louis, Missouri. Neither of us had ever been to Nashville. So we bought a laminated map from Borders Bookstore and began praying over the city. We saw a town called Franklin and almost immediately went to see if this was the place God was leading us to. After driving around for a day and a half, we stood in the Walgreens parking lot on Old Hickory and Edmonson Pike. I looked at my wife and said, "We're going to move to Franklin." We were ready to pick up and move that day. Seven years later we moved to Franklin.

During those seven years before we moved, we would come to Franklin often and walk and pray over the land. Also during that time, our middle daughter underwent a series of surgeries. She was born with Spina Bifida, and her story is another testimony of God's power in our lives. After her recovery from those surgeries and getting other issues resolved, we were able to move to Franklin. We did not know a single soul and had no financial support of any kind. If it sounds crazy, that's because it was. But at that time, as I was praying, God dropped a phrase in my heart: "One Generation Away." So I did what anyone would do: I reserved a domain name. I also began to pray, and as I did, God took me back to a moment when my daughter was about nine years old. She was watching a documentary on Martin Luther King, lying on our living room floor, and she started to cry hysterically. I said, "Lauren, what's wrong?" She asked, "Dad, why are they spraying those brown people?" I believe that God reminded me of that moment to show me that we can be one generation away from eliminating racism. This is not a generation that doesn't see color—color is part of God's creation, and it is one of the most amazing things we have—but a generation that doesn't see skin color as a division.

I knew that if change was going to happen in our immediate context, I could not do it alone. So I started calling other churches in the area, and other local pastors started showing up—pastors from all different churches and denominations in the area. There was a group of pastors and laypeople called Empty Hands Fellowship that had been meeting on Wednesdays for years. I began attending the meeting and building relationships with other pastors in town. Denominationalism creates division. This group of men believed in the same things I did. They believed that we could be one generation away from eliminating denominationalism and even racism. But they also believed in the vision for our own community, that we could be one generation away from eliminating poverty.

That's how these things started, and then as I kept praying, God showed me more. In Franklin, we used to do a festival every year on Cinco De Mayo. My wife Elaine had gone to work for a government agency that helped pay electric and light bills and deliver commodities. There was a man from a large local food bank who would deliver bread every week. He suggested to Elaine, "Hey, you know we could deliver a truckload of food to your parking lot to help you feed people." She came home and told me, and I said, "Wow, we need food for Cinco De Mayo. A truckload of food." We did, and it was wonderful. A year later, I remember telling Elaine, "I need to call the local food bank. Cinco De Mayo is coming, and we need another truckload of food." As soon as the words got out of my mouth, my phone rang. The local food bank was calling me. I thought it must be nothing; after all I'd worked with them only once. When I got off the phone, I had a free truckload of food. Free! (We toured their facility and went through a process of paperwork so that our 501(c)(3) could become a partner agency.) I had no idea where it would lead us. Two years ago we were able to distribute 1.1 million dollars worth of food—on a 75,000 dollar budget. Only God can do that.

When we see hungry people fed and needy people cared for, this is what prophet Isaiah writes about, saying, "We will be called the repairer of the breach, the restorer of streets to dwell in." I believe that God has equipped His church to accomplish that mandate, but there are a few things that need to happen. First is commitment. I once heard a man say, "Consistency trumps commitment." But I believe that commitment leads to consistency. Consistency leads to credibility, which ultimately opens hearts and makes an impact.

I have found these things to be true in my own experience. A few years ago, we had a little bit of water hit Nashville. To say a few buildings were left with a puddle or two would be an understatement. After those devastating floods in 2010, there was a massive need for relief in the Nashville area. I remember sitting with some of my fellow pastors in the area and deciding that we needed to do something about it. The church I came from in St. Louis had also flooded in the past, filled with nine feet of water less than a year after we built it. So because I had a little bit of flood relief experience, and I had the smallest church of the group, they asked me to lead the flood relief group. My immediate response was, "Sure, why not?" My wife, on the other hand, responded, "What were you thinking?" This was another huge commitment for me to add to my plate.

But as we started the relief effort, God led me to Fourth Avenue Church of Christ, where I got to know and serve alongside an incredible group of people. Almost five years later, I still have those relationships. Every day for a year, I coordinated projects, brought sandwiches, and helped out the relief teams. It's amazing how, when a disaster happens, denominations don't matter anymore. When we truly see a dire need, we rally around the cause, regardless of petty things that used to divide us. The hard truth is we're living in a disaster right now: there are hungry people in America. There are kids going home from school with nothing to eat. It is time to set aside our differences as believers and become a part of the solution.

During my time serving in flood relief with Fourth Avenue Church of Christ, I remember many churches and groups, one being a team from The Vineyard in New Orleans, Louisiana. They got to talking about how they had done relief before at their own church after Hurricane Katrina. That is what it looks like to become part of the solution. After they had experienced a disaster of their own, they committed to be part of the solution, and it eventually led to consistency.

One Generation Away has been feeding people for about five years now. If you walked in to one of our food distributions, you would see us bag 20,000 pounds of food in a parking lot, which is hard to picture. But when all that's done, we have twenty shopping carts with a cart pusher for each one. The cart pusher guides the person receiving food to each of the tables where the bags of food are. While pushing the cart, the cart pusher begins a relationship with that recipient. If you came and volunteered with us as a cart pusher, you would find something interesting. These people receiving food have the same dreams and aspirations you do. They want their kids to go to school. They want a good job. They want to pay their bills. You start to realize that there is not much separating yourself from them. So there is one simple thing we ask each of our cart pushers to do. When they reach the car and load the groceries, our cart pushers all simply ask, "Is there anything I can pray with you about today?" In this moment, you would be amazed how your consistency has led to credibility, which then leads to people opening their hearts.

One story illustrates this point. Down in Houston, Texas, we were doing a distribution. A couple found me there, and they asked me if I was the founder of the organization. I told them I was, and they said to me, "Could we tell you a story? Our friends had to leave for their son's soccer game, but they wanted you to hear this." I agreed to listen. They told me a story of their friends who had brought their reluctant 13-year-old son to a previous food distribution. He came, kicking and screaming, but as they were driving home from that food distribution, he said something incredible. That 13-year-old boy said, "Mom and Dad, thank you for taking me here. You don't know this, but this morning I was praying that if God is real, that He would reveal Himself to me." He said, "After this food distribution, I know that God is real." A 13-year-old boy looked at all the people there, from different backgrounds, different churches, different races, all coming together, and he knew that God was real—like in Revelation, every tribe, every nation, every tongue.

So I'm not writing to tell you about a brand. This is not about the great things I have done, because I've done nothing but try to be obedient to God. I want to urge you to join the movement that I believe started two millennia ago by a man named Jesus. After His resurrection, He appeared to a small group of people, and that small group turned the world upside down. I believe that's why we're here. We're supposed to turn the world upside down. In a familiar scripture in Acts 1:8, Jesus says, *But you shall receive power when the Holy Spirit has come upon you. You shall be witnesses to me in Jerusalem and in all Judea and Samaria, and to the end of the earth.* I believe that scripture with all my heart, but the problem is that we've been reaching the ends of the earth, while we step over our neighbor. We are willing to go to Haiti, Africa, and other places with great needs, but we turn a blind eye to the person next door who doesn't know where his or her next meal is coming from; but if I read the scripture correctly, we are called to be Christ's witnesses to both. We are called to take care of our Jerusalem, signifying our church, our Judea, or our immediate community, and even our Samaria, or the region we live in, and then anything beyond that is the outermost parts of the world. But it's time, Church, that we quit stepping over people that are right next door to feed someone on another continent. This is our season, our time, our finest hour as followers of Jesus Christ. This is our opportunity to do that which needs to be done.

JUSTICE, MERCY, HUMILITY

Micah 6:6-8   With what shall I come before the Lord, And bow myself before the High God? Shall I come before Him with burnt offerings, With calves a year old? 7 Will the Lord be pleased with thousands of rams, Ten thousand rivers of oil? Shall I give my firstborn for my transgression, The fruit of my body for the sin of my soul? 8 He has shown you, O man, what is good; And what does the Lord require of you but to do justly, to love mercy, and to walk humbly with your God?

What has God shown that is good? What does He require of us? Justice, mercy, and humility. These three are scarcities in our world today, but they are essentials for the Church.

Justice

*Micah 6:8   He has shown you, O man, what is good; And what does the Lord require of you but to do **justly**, to love mercy, and to walk humbly with your God?*

God talks about justice a staggering amount throughout Scripture. The Hebrew word *mizpah* is used over 200 times in the Old Testament. If God mentions justice that often, it must be important to Him.

In the modern American mindset, typically the word *justice* brings to mind prosecution. Consequently, within the Church we speak of God as a "God of Justice," implying the sense of bringing consequences for wrongdoing. However, this is only one aspect of justice. I want to explore justice in another context.

Micah 3:1   And I said: "Hear now, O heads of Jacob, and you rulers of the house of Israel: is it not for you to know justice?"

The Prophet asks a compelling question: is it not for us to know justice? How can we do justice if we don't know what justice is? Justice is defined as a participant's rights or privileges, statutory or customary. That is one definition of justice. Here is what the psalmist has to say about justice:

Psalms 82: 3-4   Defend the poor and fatherless; do justice to the afflicted and needy. 4 Deliver the poor and needy; free them from the hand of the wicked.

This is a very different picture of justice than a courtroom and a prosecution. The psalmist demands two things: we are to defend and to deliver. There are two clear commands God gives His people: defend the poor and deliver the needy. I believe that this is a mandate for the Church. And as we continue to dive into the Scriptures, I think you are going to see that from Genesis to today, God has mandated this as our responsibility: to defend and to deliver.

This concept appears everywhere from Genesis to James, time and time again by different writers and to different audiences; I think God is pretty serious about getting this across to us! It is time to stop simply reading and talking about what should be done and to start living it. I believe that God wants us to do something. I believe with all humility that God has mandated the Church to be a front-running movement for justice in this country. The Church has done a great job seeking to defend and deliver the poor and needy across the globe, but we have neglected to do so for those in our own country. We can no longer step over our neighbors to serve the world.

Genesis 18:19   For I have known him, in order that he may command his children and his household after him, that they keep the way of the Lord, to do righteousness and justice.

In this verse, we find something interesting: justice and righteousness are paired in a way which implies that they are almost interchangeable. These two words are used synonymously many times throughout the Bible. What is the context of this passage? Abraham is about to give God His own medicine. Just as God prepares to wipe out Sodom and Gomorrah, Abraham intercedes on behalf of the cities and says, "But if there are fifty righteous would you spare that city? If there are fifty righteous, would you not perform justice, God?" Not justice by torching them—which is how we see justice—but justice by saying, "I am going to save the righteous."

Abraham gives God's own words back to Him. Our kids do this to us, too. We tell them something one day, and a few days later they turn around and hold us to what we said. That same thing happens here. God says, "Keep the way of the Lord to do righteousness and justice," and Abraham comes back, reminding Him, "Hey, God, remember when You said we should keep the way of the Lord to do righteousness and justice? Well, You need to do that right now." Abraham understood that God's justice is primarily concerned with defending and delivering before prosecuting.

Exodus 22:21-22   You shall neither mistreat a stranger nor oppress him, for you were strangers in the land of Egypt. You shall not afflict any widow or fatherless child.

Am I the only one who's ever read that and wondered why I didn't ever see this before? We are all accountable to this command. This is what He means when He says afflict: You shall not look down upon, depress, or browbeat any widow or fatherless child. If you look down, depress, or browbeat one of them in any way, and they cry at all to me, I will surely hear their cry.

There are countless ordinances that God proclaimed over His nation about justice and taking care of people; it is our responsibility. You might feel like I am belaboring this point. But I do not believe that I can emphasize this enough. I think we need to understand how important this is to God. And if it is important to Jesus, who is the head of the Church, then we ought to be doing it.

Deuteronomy 10:17-18   For the Lord your God is God of gods and Lord of lords, the great God, mighty and awesome, who shows no partiality nor takes a bribe. 18 He administers justice for the fatherless and the widow, and loves the stranger, giving him food and clothing.

He administers justice for the fatherless and the widow, and loves the stranger, giving him food and clothing. In my own church, we have been discussing these issues. We have talked a lot particularly about immigration. Strangers in our land. I hear professing Christians say things like, "Kick 'em out! That's what we ought to do!" Wrong. God says to take care of the stranger.

He goes on to say, in fact, if a stranger comes into your land, you are to treat him the same as your own, and he would do the same things you do.

Deuteronomy 15:7-11 If there is among you a poor man of your brethren, within any of the gates in your land which the Lord your God is giving you, you shall not harden your heart nor shut your hand from your poor brother, 8 but you shall open your hand wide to him and willingly lend him sufficient for his need, whatever he needs. 9 Beware lest there be a wicked thought in your heart, saying, 'The seventh year, the year of release, is at hand,' and your eye be evil against your poor brother and you give him nothing, and he cry out to the Lord against you, and it become sin among you. 10 You shall surely give to him, and your heart should not be grieved when you give to him, because for this thing the Lord your God will bless you in all your works and in all to which you put your hand. 11 For the poor will never cease from the land; therefore I command you, saying, 'You shall open your hand wide to your brother, to your poor and your needy, in your land.'

Here is an answer in scripture for anyone who has ever said, "I don't want to give that person money, because who knows what he will use it for?" That's not your problem. Right here the scripture tells you that is not your problem. God says to open your hand to the needy. It is not your responsibility whether that person goes and buys drugs with it, or buys beer with it, or anything else. Your job and mine is to open our hand to the needy. Give. No stipulations, no exceptions. Give!

Part of the reason I am so convicted about this issue is because God is so explicit about it. God is never vague when talking about caring for the poor.

15

Proverbs 14:31   He who oppresses the poor reproaches his Maker, But he who honors Him has mercy on the needy.

Isaiah 1:17   Learn to do good; seek justice, rebuke the oppressor; defend the fatherless, plead for the widow.

Matthew 22:38-39   This is the first and great commandment. 39 And the second is like it: 'You shall love your neighbor as yourself.'

I am a firm believer that it is hard to "love your neighbor as yourself" if you don't love yourself. And the problem with so many people is they are so disappointed in themselves that they can't show the love of Christ because they don't even like or love who they are. Tim Keller writes in his book *Generous Justice* that to walk in God's grace, we must do justice.[1] The level in which you experience God's grace is the maximum level you can distribute justice. If this is true, it is a scary thought because it suggests that the church has not fully received (or embraced) the grace of God. We are very limited in the amount of justice we want to give. The opportunities for justice and grace are all around.

Matthew 25:35-40   For I was hungry and you gave Me food; I was thirsty and you gave Me drink; I was a stranger and you took Me in; 36 I was naked and you clothed Me; I was sick and you visited Me; I was in prison and you came to Me. 37 Then the righteous will answer Him, saying, 'Lord, when did we see You hungry and feed You, or thirsty and give You drink? 38 When did we see You a stranger and take You in, or naked and clothe You? 39 Or

---

1. Timothy Keller, *Generous Justice: How God's Grace Makes Us Just* (New York: Penguin Group, 2010), 120.

when did we see You sick, or in prison, and come to You?'
40 And the King will answer and say to them, 'Assuredly,
I say to you, inasmuch as you did it to one of the least of
these My brethren, you did it to Me.'

The ministry I founded has done a lot of food distributions. Being completely honest, we've all looked at somebody and thought, "What are you doing in this line?" Or we take their food to their car and think, "My gosh, you're driving this car and you need free food?" We all make judgments, but our natural tendency is not to give justice.

I was at a distribution once, talking to the pastor and looking at the people in the line. He was telling me what he had been preaching on in his church, and I shared with him that I was preparing to preach on justice. I told him, "Right there in that line are 300 representations of Jesus." When did I see you, Jesus? When I was hungry, when I was in a prison cell, when I didn't have any clothes. It shows our level of grace when we look across the table and make judgments about who deserves to receive help. That shows that we have not comprehended the fullness of the grace of God.

English reformer John Bradford, wrongly imprisoned in the Tower of London, is said to have seen a group of prisoners being led to execution and observed, "There but for the grace of God I go." When your grace meter is low, all it takes is to understand that you own nothing, you literally are a steward of everything, and it is only God's grace that keeps you from walking to your own execution. There is nothing but Jesus Christ in you, the hope of glory. Jesus Christ crucified, risen from the dead. That's all that you represent and that's who you are.

Paul calls himself the chief among sinners. Our reaction is often, "Paul, you're the chief sinner? Give me a break; you're just saying that." No, he isn't. He had experienced the grace of God to such a degree that he understood, "I am the chief of all sinners.

I am the least worthy to be an apostle." But for the grace of God. This also means if it weren't for the *justice* of God, we wouldn't be here right now. He would have wiped out humanity. And once again, not justice like a guilty verdict and a sentence, but that God would say, "My compassion and mercy so overwhelm me that although my heart is to wipe out these ungrateful stiff-necked people, I must honor what I have committed to and give them justice."

> *James 2:1-4   My brethren, do not hold the faith of our Lord Jesus Christ, the Lord of glory, with partiality. 2 For if there should come into your assembly a man with gold rings, in fine apparel, and there should also come in a poor man in filthy clothes, 3 and you pay attention to the one wearing the fine clothes and say to him, "You sit here in a good place," and say to the poor man, "You stand there," or, "Sit here at my footstool," 4 have you not shown partiality among yourselves, and become judges with evil thoughts?*

If I am being honest, these are thoughts I have had when certain people have walked into my church. "Man, I wonder how big a tithe check he is going to write. That guy, I bet he could fund everything we need to do for the rest of year. I wonder how many trucks of food that guy could buy? Man, look at him, I bet he could really do something for us." These thoughts are offensive to God. I need to repent for being carnal.

I pray that I don't care who walks through that door, whether they have tattoos or piercings or whatever else. About your judgment where God said, "Don't pierce," the justice of God is that God died for that pierced person, that tattooed person, the smelly, homeless person. Christ died for that person. As much as He died for you, He died for them. When our judgment says that those people have nothing to offer us, God's justice shows us that they have everything to offer. They help us experience that immense grace that God poured upon us. We experience grace by extending it to others. Freely you have received, freely give.

James 2:5-8   Listen, my beloved brethren: Has God not chosen the poor of this world to be rich in faith and heirs of the kingdom which He promised to those who love Him? 6 But you have dishonored the poor man. Do not the rich oppress you and drag you into the courts? 7 Do they not blaspheme that noble name by which you are called? 8 If you really fulfill the royal law according to the Scripture, "You shall love your neighbor as yourself," you do well.

So here we are: Deuteronomy, Micah, Matthew, and James all say that if you show partiality, you commit sin. For us to ignore the poor is to blaspheme. Is this sin in God's eyes the same as adultery, the same as murder, all the things you think are so horrific? Guess what? Ignoring the poor, put it on the list. This is not easy to hear, but it is in God's word, time and time again.

Mercy

*Micah 6:8   He has shown you, O man, what is good; and what does the Lord require of you but to do justly, to love **mercy**, and to walk humbly with your God?*

God instructs us to do justly, but He also calls us to love mercy. Often we love mercy for ourselves but want to see "justice" done for others. We cast judgment on the world but expect to receive mercy ourselves.

James 2:13 For judgment is without mercy to the one who has shown no mercy. Mercy triumphs over judgment.

Wrongly interpreted, this idea can become a slippery slope—mercy triumphs over judgment—and we end up with what some have jokingly called "sloppy agape" love; in other words, God doesn't want you to be holy; He just wants you to be happy. But the Bible still says that mercy triumphs over judgment. His mercies are new every morning. When we make our judgment bigger than our mercy, we often convey this message: change your life and then come to God. God's message has always been, "Come as you are."

At our food distributions, people in line often ask, "Can I come to your church?" And I've said, "Of course you can," to which I often receive the response, "Well, I don't have nice clothes, so I don't think I can come to church." That is what they know about church. In regard to our church, that is a total misconception. But there are still people out there who think they need to wear the right clothes and have the right lifestyle to even enter the doors of a church.

This concerns the Church as a whole, but it should also challenge us on a personal level: would you be willing to sit next to somebody who hasn't been able to bathe in weeks? What about if that person had alcohol on his or her breath? Would you be willing to sit next to a homosexual couple? These are real issues for Christians and for the Church. Which is greater, our mercy or our judgments? I do not want my church to be a place where we give people front row seats if they are rich or famous; I'd rather give the "best seats" to those people I just described. I want those people to be celebrated, to come in and know that God loves them and has a plan for their lives.

We talked about how if you show partiality, you commit sin. So for us to show mercy, we have to first understand that we have received mercy.

Ephesians 2:8-9 For by grace you have been saved through faith, and that not of yourselves; it is the gift of God, 9 not of works, lest anyone should boast.

Not to burst your bubble, but it is by *grace* you have been saved through faith. It's not because you earned it. It's not because you got all the gold stars. It's not because you memorize the most Bible verses. It's not because you know this or that! It is by grace that you have been saved through faith, not of works lest any man should boast. When we come in contact with people, whether it is at food distributions or toy distributions or other avenues of service to our communities, we must always remember this truth. You didn't earn your salvation or position with God, so don't expect others—especially the poor—to earn theirs.

Our culture is prone to see the poor and think, "Well, they should just get a job or pull themselves up by their bootstraps." The truth is that you did not pull yourself up by your bootstraps. *By grace you have been saved.* Your good works, your righteous deeds, your holiness, not even your 80 hours of work per week or your big bank account, none of that matters in God's eyes. If we truly realized that we did not earn anything we have, we would be the most humble, generous, and sacrificial people on earth.

Luke 10:29-37 "And who is my neighbor?" Sometimes we don't ask the question because we don't want the answer. Jesus answers, *"A certain man went down from Jerusalem to Jericho, and fell among thieves, who stripped him of his clothing, wounded him, and departed, leaving him half dead. But a certain Samaritan, as he journeyed, came where he was. And when he saw him, he had compassion. So he went to him and bandaged his wounds, pouring on oil and wine; and he set him on his own animal, brought him to an inn, and took care of him. On the next day, when he departed, he took out two denarii, gave them to the innkeeper, and said to him, 'Take care of him; and whatever more you spend, when I come again, I will repay you.' So which of these three do you think was neighbor to him who fell among the thieves?" And he said, "He who showed mercy on him." Then Jesus said to him, "Go and do likewise."*

Go and do likewise. These four words should pierce your heart. Jesus is speaking to a Jew, who considers Samaritans the same as dogs. And in Jesus' story, two "good Jews" of the Levitical priesthood ignore and pass by this suffering person. Then a "dog" walks by, picks the man up, cleans him, puts him up in a nice hotel and says, "Here's some extra money for anything else you might need. And if anything more happens, let me know and I will pay that too."

Most of us err on the side of, "What is the least I can give for them to get by?" So when we give, we think we need to get more information about them so they don't get more than they should. Thank God that He does not show mercy like we do. This is not to say that a little vetting is wrong, but when our vetting becomes bigger than our mercy, we have an issue. That means our judgments are bigger than our mercy. We quickly forget the mercy that was shown to us, and our judgments are skewed.

We are one of the wealthiest nations on the planet, and we give more than any other nation. That is wonderful. I firmly believe we need to go to Africa, Asia, Haiti, and other places that have seen devastation and poverty. Great need exists all over the earth, and the Church should be leading the movement to mobilize and send people to those places. But we must quit stepping over our neighbor in need to meet a need on the other side of the world. We can no longer leave our Jerusalem to go to Samaria and the uttermost parts of the earth. Then we become just like the religious men in Jesus' story, passing over the person in need on our way to do something more "holy" and "important." And then we end up with a black eye in our communities because we are not serving the very people next door. When Jesus says go into Jerusalem, Judea, Samaria, and the uttermost parts of the world, He is not asking to pick which ones we want to go to. We cannot neglect one to do the other.

Deuteronomy 24:14-15 You shall not oppress a hired servant who is poor and needy, whether one of your brethren or one of the aliens who is in your land within your gates. 15 Each day you shall give him his wages, and not let the sun go down on it, for he is poor and has set his heart on it; lest he cry out against you to the Lord, and it be sin to you.

This passage deals with employers and the poor that work for them. But if it is a sin for employers to mistreat the poor, I believe that it is a sin for the Church to mistreat the poor. I have been in church for 27 years now, and I cannot remember the last time I heard somebody preach that oppressing the poor is sin. I have heard a lot things preached as sin, but that's not one of them.

We have to be careful of this, because the poor aren't just people who don't have money. People come to church because they are poor in spirit. They have needs. When people who are poor walk through the doors of our churches (they are coming in because they are poor in something), we need to be attentive to their needs. We need to break away from our comfortable little groups, because there are poor people walking into our churches every single week. Whether they are poor financially or poor in Spirit, they are coming open and willing to receive the love of Christ. And they need God's people to reach out and help them.

Jesus calls these people blessed. "Blessed are the poor in spirit." Jesus says, "The poor you will have with you always." I believe that this is one of the greatest issues the Church will face over the next decade: how will we deal with the poor among us? So far, we have largely failed.

Our gut response is, "My gosh, Pastor, what else do you want us to do? We feed people, we give away toys, and we are doing all these things." The Bible says that those who are like God are actively compassionate. Mercy is a little more than just programs and charities. Mercy is being actively compassionate toward people who visit your church. It is being actively compassionate in the grocery store, and at work every day. It is seeking out those who are poor in spirit—seeking out those who are needy and hungry.

This is not a government issue. The government cannot do this alone. They cannot feed the world and take care of the poor and the needy; they were never called to. This is not socialism. It is not capitalism. It is not communism. It is justice. It is mercy.

Humility

*Micah 6:8   He has shown you, O man, what is good; and what does the Lord require of you but to do justly, to love mercy, and to walk **humbly** with your God?*

The Bible calls King David a man after God's own heart. But it wasn't because David was the most well-behaved or obedient. It was because King David had a humble heart. I am beginning to learn that to practice God's justice to serve the poor—which is our responsibility, as we have discussed—we must humble ourselves and realize that we are no different than the people we serve. I am no different than them, but for the grace of God, I go. The moment our judgments say, "Why are you here? You should get a better job, or you ought to do this or do that," we have to resist that temptation steadfastly in the faith. But for the grace of God, I go.

So as we consider our justice and mercy, we must also consider our humility. The only way to serve someone else is to be humble. And we may find that our humility will rub off on those around us.

Luke 11:39 Then the Lord said to him, "Now you Pharisees make the outside of the cup and dish clean, but your inward part is full of greed and wickedness."

This is something at which Christians excel. We clean up on the outside. We go to church. We have bumper stickers that tell you we go to church. We wear cross necklaces and t-shirts to let everyone know, but often our lives look no different than the world.

This inward-focused attitude affects our service. We start to think, "Can you believe the people who come here in this line are not even thankful that we are giving them food? How dare they not thank me! Can't they see how clean and selfless I am?" Well, those people must have x-ray vision, because they usually see right through that self-righteous attitude to what is really going on beneath. I suspect that often the people we serve with a self-righteous attitude can see clearly that we are no better than them—in fact in some ways we're a lot worse.

Luke 11:42 For you tithe mint and rue and all manner of herbs, and pass by justice and the love of God. These you ought to have done, without leaving the others undone.

These you ought to have done without leaving the others undone. So you should keep tithing and you should not pass by people and not give them justice. What Jesus means by justice is you ought to meet their need when you pass by them. "Well, how do I know if I give that guy money, he's not going to go by alcohol?" I don't know. That's not your problem. It's not your job to figure out what to do with the money you give them. It's your job to take care of people. It is God's job to judge them on what they do with it. I'm sorry, it just is. It causes us not to perform justice. We consider it justice when we think, "Well, I didn't give to him because they're sinners and I know they're going to go get drunk with it and by golly, I'm going to judge them for God. I'm going to take care of that judgment right now and I won't give them anything," when God would say, "You know what? You give to them and I'll take care of judging them." Last time I checked He didn't send Chris Whitney into the world to judge the world of sin. He did not send Chris Whitney into the world so that he could lead people to God. That was called the Holy Spirit, and Chris Whitney, in the Greek, Hebrew, Aramaic, pick any language you want, does not translate into the Holy Spirit last time I checked. He did send me and you to tell people about Him with our actions and if necessary our words. So let the Holy Ghost do His job. It's okay, He'll figure it out.

> *Luke 14:11-12 "For whoever exalts himself will be humbled, and he who humbles himself will be exalted."*
> *Then He also said to him who invited Him, "When you give a dinner or a supper, do not ask your friends, your brothers, your relatives, nor rich neighbors, lest they also invite you back, and you be repaid. But when you give a feast, invite the poor, the maimed, the lame, the blind. And you will be blessed, because they cannot repay you; for you shall be repaid at the resurrection of the just."*

I have a pastor friend named Kevin Riggs, and something his church does has convicted me. Once a quarter they host a family meal for their community, and they simply invite everyone.

They pass out flyers in the community, and many of his church members come to serve. But they do not invite only people who are going to contribute to the meal. Isn't that a novel idea? The church hosts a meal for people who actually might need a meal. The message this sends from the Church to the community is a powerful one: it is not about what you can bring, but it is about what we have all been given.

But when you give a feast, invite the poor, the maimed, the lame, the blind.

Every year my Church hosts a Super Bowl party, not necessarily because of the game, but because of the opportunity for fellowship. We have free food and the game on the big screens. This past year, I was reading this passage and realized I should repent. We as a church could have gone to places with people in great need and extended the invitation to enjoy that free food and fellowship. This makes some of us very uncomfortable, but this is the calling of the church to the least of the least, the lowest of the low. That party could have been an opportunity to reach out to someone for the first time. I praise the Lord that there are people in my church that have a heart for the poor more than I sometimes do.

What this comes down to is an issue of humility. We want to feel comfortable in church with people just like us. We want to have the cleanest and newest facilities, and we feel safe when everyone looks and dresses like us. But that is not what God calls us to. He says that when we throw a party, we are not to invite those who are going to help us climb the social ladder or those who will give the largest donation. We are to humble ourselves and offer what we have to those who truly need it.

James 4:6–10 "God resists the proud, but gives grace to the humble." 7 Therefore submit to God. Resist the devil and he will flee from you. 8 Draw near to God and He will draw near to you. Cleanse your hands, you sinners; and purify your hearts, you double-minded. 9 Lament and mourn and weep! Let your laughter be turned to mourning and your joy to gloom. 10 Humble yourselves in the sight of the Lord, and He will lift you up.

Pride comes before destruction. God resists the proud but gives grace to the humble. A haughty spirit before a fall. I can think of too many times in my life when I was so proud, so haughty, so arrogant. Thank God, my wife stayed around me. Thank God, people would still talk to me. Honestly, I feel like I have to work on this every day. Every day I pray, "God, help me not to be prideful." Part of my personality is that I am just a teeny bit passionate. I think that can sometimes come across as arrogance. So I have to work on not coming across as arrogant, just because I am passionate about something. I have to admit that I don't know much, but I know that I need to draw near to God, so He will draw near to me.

"Submit to God, resist the devil and he must flee." I love that part of this passage, because it gives us confidence. See, if we are willing to submit our lives to God, we can resist the devil, and he *must* flee! He has no choice. This isn't an option for him. He has to go. Now, the part that gets challenging for us is *submitting* to God.

1 Peter 5:5-9 Likewise you younger people, submit yourselves to your elders. Yes, all of you be submissive to one another, and be clothed with humility, for "God resists the proud, but gives grace to the humble." 6 Therefore humble yourselves under the mighty hand of God, that He may exalt you in due time, 7 casting all your care upon Him, for He cares for you. 8 Be sober, be vigilant; because

*your adversary the devil walks about like a roaring lion,
seeking whom he may devour. 9 Resist him, steadfast in
the faith, knowing that the same sufferings are experienced
by your brotherhood in the world.*

Once again we are back to humbling ourselves: "Casting all
your care upon Him, for He cares for you." I have come to figure
out that I can't fix a lot of things. I've tried; I thought I could. I
thought I could fix people. I thought I could fix stuff. But I have
come to realize that I need to "humble myself under the mighty
hand of God, casting all my care upon Him." The attitude of
society is, "I can fix this." "I can handle that." "I know what I
am doing." "I have it under control." We must get past that, to
humble ourselves and stand before God and say, "God, I have
no clue."

The text tells us to "clothe yourself with humility." Imagine
the picture of getting up in the morning and dressing yourself
with humility. It is not our natural state or posture. You might
know all the answers, but why don't you clothe yourself in
humility and not worry about giving them unless someone asks
for them? Maybe God wants somebody to step up and learn
what you already know. Don't worry about being seen or heard;
just clothe yourself with humility. Cast all your cares on the
Lord, for He cares for you. God will call you to the front when
He is ready and when He wants to. He will establish you when
He wants to establish you and draw you out when He wants you
to be drawn out.

We have to be careful not to start reading our own press
clippings too much. We start to overlook what really
matters. We are starting to pick out who is "taking advantage
of us" or who "doesn't deserve our help." I understand that to
an extent there is wise stewardship, but a lot of that is not our

responsibility. That is between them and God. Without humility, our judgment always grows bigger than our mercy. It can reach the point where our judgments of someone end up with us robbing from a widow, inadvertently. We have to be careful not to think we can't become like that. We hear people say negative things about certain churches and in our haughtiness and in our arrogance we think, "I would never do that." In those times, we need to remember, "But for the grace of God, I go."

I COMMIT

2 Timothy 4:1, 5   I charge you therefore before God and the Lord Jesus Christ, who will judge the living and the dead at His appearing and His kingdom: 5 But you be watchful in all things, endure afflictions, do the work of an evangelist, fulfill your ministry.

I've been told that I need to be committed—but that's not the kind of "committed" I want to talk about in this chapter. I want to talk about being committed to what we believe. I believe that Paul is talking to Timothy about commitment; that is why he ends with the charge, "fulfill your ministry." Beginning in ministry is great, but fulfilling it takes commitment. Amen? And commitment is not easy. He writes in verse 2 to convince, rebuke, exhort. These are heavy responsibilities. These are things that we must be sure to temper with an attitude of love, lest we wound our brothers and sisters in the process. This is why you are called to remove the plank from your own eye before you remove the speck from your brother's. Convince, rebuke, exhort, and fulfill your ministry.

Committing in Trials

> *1 Peter 4:12, 14   Beloved, do not think it strange concerning the fiery trial which is to try you, as though some strange thing happened to you; 14 If you are reproached for the name of Christ, blessed are you, for the Spirit of glory and of God rests upon you.*

So many Christians are shocked when the world attacks them for their faith. This shouldn't be a surprise to us; they crucified Jesus! But this text tells us it is a blessing if we are reproached for the name of Jesus. On their part He is blasphemed, but on your part He is glorified. You are not even the one being blasphemed. Sorry, but you're not that important. But even as the world tries to blaspheme Him, on your part He is being glorified. You bring glory and honor to God when you stand strong in the face of persecution and stay committed.

> *1 Peter 4:16-19   Yet if anyone suffers as a Christian, let him not be ashamed, but let him glorify God in this matter. 17 For the time has come for judgment to begin at the house of God; and if it begins with us first, what will be the end of those who do not obey the gospel of God? 18 Now "If the righteous one is scarcely saved, where will the ungodly and the sinner appear?" 19 Therefore let those who suffer according to the will of God commit their souls to Him in doing good, as to a faithful Creator.*

This is vital to understand. If bad things happen to you, it does not necessarily mean that you are a bad person or that you missed God. In fact, you will likely find that sometimes when you obey God, things happen. If I look across the street at a hornet's nest and say, "That doesn't bother me in the least bit,"

I probably will not get stung. But if I cross the street, pick up a stick, and hit the hornet's nest, I might find myself less safe and comfortable. It is time that we as Christians pick up sticks and start hitting the enemy's hornet's nests. We can no longer stand by as he preys on those who are totally defenseless against his devices.

2 Timothy 1:12 For this reason I also suffer these things; nevertheless I am not ashamed, for I know whom I have believed and am persuaded that He is able to keep what I have committed to Him until that Day.

The main reason we can be committed to God is because He is committed to us. You can trust that if you commit your life to God, He will keep you until the day He returns or until the day you blast into eternity. You can be confident that if you commit to Him, He will take care of you.

James 1:2-4 My brethren, count it all joy when you fall into various trials, 3 knowing that the testing of your faith produces patience. 4 But let patience have its perfect work, that you may be perfect and complete, lacking nothing.

Being committed takes a level of maturity. When James talks about being perfect and complete, he has in mind this idea of being mature. When I was a youth pastor, I always advised students not to pursue dating relationships. "But I am in love!" No, you're not. At that point in life, most of us simply do not have the maturity to commit our lives to another human being yet. Most of us aren't even mature enough to remember deodorant every day or to clean our rooms. Before we can be committed, we have to be mature enough to understand the cost of that commitment. James explains that maturity comes through facing trials.

Committing Everything

*Luke 21:4   For all these out of their abundance have put
in offerings for God, but she out of her poverty put in all
the livelihood that she had.*

Jesus tells a story of a poor elderly woman who, in the midst
of rich men making significant financial contributions at the
temple, gives the last bit of money she has. That is commitment.
We give 10 percent and think we are committed. God wants
everything. He does not need our money, but He wants our trust.

When Elaine was pregnant with our second child, in the
26th week we had a blood test done and discovered that
our child had Spina Bifida. We were devastated. The doctors
wanted to keep doing tests, but we told them, "No. No more
tests. We are going to stand and trust God for complete healing."
In no way did we deny that the mountain was there, but we stood
on God's word, which says that when we speak to the mountain
it must move.

A few months went by as we encouraged one another, both
of us having bad days, but by the grace of God not at the same
time. One day I came home from work and Elaine said, "We
need to go see R.W. Schambach." Elaine had never even heard of
this man, but she felt God had put him on her heart. If you have
never heard him, just listen to his program once and he will blow
your mind. His famous line was, "You don't have trouble! All you
need is faith in God."

If you knew Elaine, you would know that she is not one who
flippantly says she has heard from God. So I knew I better listen.
Elaine proceeded to tell me that she felt like she was supposed
to write a letter to Schambach, so she called to get his address
and a lady told her, almost laughing at Elaine for being so naïve

to believe that R.W. Schambach would actually read it himself. She told Elaine that he gets thousands of letters a day, and he has prayer teams that read the letters and pray over them. She sent it anyway, in obedience.

A few weeks later we went to Chicago to hear Schambach speak. We didn't have any money, but Dave, my boss at the time, was willing to take us. So he and his wife drove us in their minivan and paid our way to go to Chicago. When we arrived, our friends told us to go talk to him. We had never given any money to Schambach, and as far as we knew, he had no idea who we were, but they urged us to go talk to him. We said, "No way." And Dave responded, "You've got to be kidding me. We just drove 300 miles; you can walk 50 feet to go say something to the guy."

We mustered up the courage to go talk to him. I remember standing in front of Schambach, a prominent man, over six feet tall, a widely-known speaker and evangelist. Elaine stuck out her hand and said, "Um, hi...I'm Elaine Whitney." He grabbed her hand, pulled her close to him, and said, "You're the one that wrote the letter." We were astonished. The guy gets thousands of letters a day. Elaine, in disbelief, asked, "You read it?" He answered, "Not only did I read it, I brought it with me," patting his chest pocket. "You believe God for a miracle tonight, because He is going to heal your baby!"

We may have walked back to our seats—or we may have floated; we don't know how we got back. But we were sitting in the fourth row, which was the first one available to the public. Schambach began to deliver a tremendous testimony about a lady who was broke and used all the money she had to get to an A.A. Allen revival meeting in Kentucky. Schambach worked as an intern for Allen at the time. This woman had come to the revival because her child was born with 24 different deformities. She had only 20 dollars to her name—just enough for gas to get back home. At these types of revivals, A.A. Allen always took up an offering, and at that moment this woman bolted out of her seat. She sprinted to the altar and gave the last 20 dollars she had to her name. That was all she had to get home. That is commitment.

Schambach told how A.A. Allen asked everyone to close their eyes. Here was a child born without a tongue, dumb and blind, with club feet. A.A. Allen said, "We are going to pray and believe God for a miracle." In Schambach's telling of the story, he recalled, "I wasn't closing my eyes! Are you kidding me? I wasn't going to miss this for anything; I wanted to see this miracle!" As they prayed for this child, he watched feet grow. Four years old, this child had never spoken. A tongue formed in his mouth. His eyes turned like blue cesspools and lit up. And they put him down and watched him run across the stage and cry, "Mama!" That is the God we serve.

After preaching this message, Schambach announced, "There is a couple here from St. Louis. The woman is pregnant, and the baby has been diagnosed with a serious condition, so we are going to lay hands on them and believe that God is going to do a miracle." He called us up to the front and had all the pastors who were there agree in prayer. He also asked everyone in the building to stand and hold hands. "But before you do, ask that person if they believe in miracles, and if they say they do not, don't hold their hands, because God is going to perform a miracle tonight!" He himself laid his hands on Elaine's belly and began to pray over her, the baby, and myself. I believe in the power of agreement in prayer.

We went back to our seats, and they immediately began to take up the offering. Guess how much money I had in my pocket? Twenty dollars to get home from Chicago. St. Louis is a long way away, and I had 20 dollars to get home. As the offering baskets circulated, I leaned over to Elaine, telling her that I felt like God was telling me to donate the 20 dollars I had in my pocket. She said, "I do, too." Then I had a brilliant idea.

I asked Dave's wife, "Hey, Melody, would you write us a check for 20 dollars so we can put it in the offering? All we have is 20 dollars cash, and if we give it we won't have anything when we get home." I am not proud of this moment. I consider this one of the most embarrassing things I have ever done in my life. But she wrote the check, and we put it in the offering bucket. Suddenly, someone tapped me on the arm. We didn't know anyone else there, so I looked over thinking, "What do you want?" This man held out a fist, and he dropped a 20-dollar bill in my hands. I simultaneously felt like praising God and kicking myself.

I tell you that story to show that I do not always get it right, but God is still faithful. It does not mean you need to go quit your job or give away everything you have, but we all know we have a little more we can give, and we all hold onto things we haven't entrusted to God. I wish I had been like the woman in Jesus' parable or the woman from Schambach's story. God is always faithful; He just wants us to trust Him.

Matthew 19:16-22   Now behold, one came and said to Him, "Good Teacher, what good thing shall I do that I may have eternal life?" 17 So He said to him, "Why do you call Me good? No one is good but One, that is, God. But if you want to enter into life, keep the commandments." 18 He said to Him, "Which ones?" Jesus said, "'You shall not murder,' 'You shall not commit adultery,' 'You shall not steal,' 'You shall not bear false witness,' 19 'Honor your father and your mother,' and, 'You shall love your neighbor as yourself.'" 20 The young man said to Him, "All these things I have kept from my youth. What do I still lack?" 21 Jesus said to him, "If you want to be perfect, go, sell what you have and give to the poor, and you will have treasure in heaven; and come, follow Me." 22 But when the young man heard that saying, he went away sorrowful, for he had great possessions.

Verse 20 contains a great question from this young man. What do I still lack? He knows he has obeyed all 10 of the Commandments, so he thinks he must be in. I'm not sure if he is ready when the answer hits: sell everything you have, give it to the poor, and follow Me. The Luke 21 woman gave a few coins' commitment: through the roof. The rich young man's commitment: below the floor. What a contrast in commitment levels! This is not meant to discourage us but to challenge us. You don't have to have much to be fully committed.

The Commitment of Jesus

Matthew 26:42   Again, a second time, He went away and prayed, saying, "O My Father, if this cup cannot pass away from Me unless I drink it, Your will be done."

That is commitment. We all know it was the only way, but even Jesus wrestled with it. Remember that, because that means it is okay to struggle with our commitment. But the bottom line is to stay committed. Jesus struggled with His commitment. "If this cup cannot pass away from me unless I drink it, Your will be done." In the end, He was committed to the will of the Father above all else.

I told you about my tremendous failure to be committed to God during the offering in Chicago. There is a man in the Bible named Peter who struggled with his commitment, too.

John 21:15   So when they had eaten breakfast, Jesus said to Simon Peter, "Simon, son of Jonah, do you love Me more than these?" He said to Him, "Yes, Lord; You know that I love You." He said to him, "Feed My lambs."

You might think this is no big deal. Jesus is challenging Peter because Peter just denied Him three times. You remember the story where Peter denies Him three times? And we also remember the other story: Jesus asks, "Simon Bar-Jonah, who do you say that I am?" Peter replies, "I say that you are the Christ, the Son of the Living God." "Simon Bar-Jonah, blessed are you among men, and upon this rock I will build my church, for that came from my heavenly Father." A few verses later, Peter spews, "You can't die! Are you kidding?" And Jesus rebukes him, "Get behind me, Satan!" Peter had a way of putting his foot in his mouth, but he also had a way of hearing God's voice. Peter promises, "I would never deny you, Lord." Jesus corrects him: "You will deny me three times before the rooster crows." And he does.

That brings us to this passage. Jesus has risen from the dead, and standing before Peter, He says, "Peter, do you love me?" And when Jesus says that, He uses the term *agape* love—unconditionally committing every fiber of your being. The sacrificial kind of love. And Peter answers, "I love you." Peter answers with *phileo* love, a friendship love.

John 21:16   He said to him again a second time, "Simon, son of Jonah, do you love Me?" He said to Him, "Yes, Lord; You know that I love You."

Once again Jesus asks him, "Do you *agape* (unconditionally) love me?" He replies, "Yes, Lord you know that I *phileo* (contingently) love you." Jesus replies, "Tend My sheep."

17   He said to him the third time, "Simon, son of Jonah, do you love Me?"

This time Jesus speaks to Peter at his own level. He demonstrates the redemptive love of God by using Peter's terminology. He asks if Peter *phileo* loves him. And that gives Peter the opportunity to answer. Peter, clearly grieved, responds, "Lord, You know all things; You know that I love You." And Jesus says, "Feed My sheep."

Despite my inability to commit to God with that silly 20-dollar bill that was in my pocket, God, in His redeeming mercy and grace, allowed me another day to make it right and to commit my life to Him. Look what He says in verse 18.

John 21:18-19   Most assuredly, I say to you, when you were younger, you girded yourself and walked where you wished; but when you are old, you will stretch out your hands, and another will gird you and carry you where you do not wish." 19 This He spoke, signifying by what death he would glorify God. And when He had spoken this, He said to him, "Follow Me."

Matthew 4:18-19   And Jesus, walking by the Sea of Galilee, saw two brothers, Simon called Peter, and Andrew his brother, casting a net into the sea; for they were fishermen. 19 Then He said to them, "Follow Me."

How good is God? The disciples have heard Jesus say, "Follow me and I will make you fishers of men." And now here we are at the end of John 21, and Jesus looks again at Peter and says, "I know that your commitment has waivered and failed." But He invites him again, "Follow Me." From the first day you encounter Jesus until your last breath, through all your highs and lows, He is calling you to the same thing: "Follow Me."

Commitment is not a one-time deal. You must renew your commitment day by day, moment by moment, because you will waver in your commitment. That does not make you weak

—it just makes you human. And if you blow your commitment, Jesus invites you again to follow Him. Peter is one who left everything, his livelihood, his fishing net, his family, all to follow Jesus. Surely Peter thought, "I'm all in." But Peter wasn't all in. That is where we have to be honest with ourselves. Sometimes we think we are all in, but we really still aren't sure. But when we realize and confess, "Lord, I repent, because I talk a better game than I live," Jesus will come back and say, "Do you love me? Feed my sheep." He will even break it down to your level. He knows what you can handle. And then He will say, "Follow me."

SERVING WITH BALANCE

Matthew 20:28 Just as the Son of Man did not come to be served, but to serve, and to give His life a ransom for many.

I thought we probably ought to address this subject: why serve? If Jesus came to serve then that was enough reason right there. And I believe that if you truly lived four chapters of the Bible you would make the greatest impact of any Christian to walk the planet. Three of those are Matthew 5, 6, and 7, the fourth being Isaiah 58. In fact, there was an old preacher who said if whatever you preach is not involved with Matthew 5, 6, and 7, then you are probably wasting your breath.

> *Matthew 5:13-16 You are the salt of the earth; but if the salt loses its flavor, how shall it be seasoned? It is then good for nothing but to be thrown out and trampled underfoot by men. 14 You are the light of the world. A city that is set on a hill cannot be hidden. 15 Nor do they light a lamp and put it under a basket, but on a lampstand, and it gives light to all who are in the house. 16 Let your light so shine before men, that they may see your good works and glorify your Father in heaven.*

We spend much of our time in what I call "Ditch Christianity." We do everything in extremes, and we end up off in the ditch on either side. For example we say, "It is not about works, so I am not going to do anything for God." We get off into a ditch of no works. Obviously that's crazy, not doing anything for God, so we get out of the ditch and drive on the road for a while. Then our attitude starts to become all about works. "We've got to work, work, work. We've got to earn God's love." Now we're off in another ditch. So we've got to learn some balance.

Balance is not a bad word. If you don't balance the tires on your car, your ride is going to be bumpy. Have you ever gotten into a car and it feels like the front end is shaking off, and you think, "I need new tie rods..." or something else painfully expensive? Then you go into the tire place and they say, "For five bucks we'll put a little weight on the front and it will be fine." You think, "You're kidding me? I thought my front end was going to fall off!" They add a tiny metal piece to your front tire, and all of a sudden the entire car no longer shakes. That is what I want to talk about: bringing balance into our lives so that we can move forward in our service more smoothly and efficiently. Then we can be a light to our world, and our good works will glorify our Father who is in Heaven.

Why do we serve? So we can be the light of the world. This can be really challenging for a human being. If I am being honest, I wrestle with this quite a bit, especially doing a lot of distributions and giving away a lot of food; we feed a lot of people. So I am calling news stations, reporters, and inside I am thinking, "Well, that is drawing attention to me." I do not intend to draw attention to us, but I do want to draw attention to a desperate need in our society—that we have people who are starving; literally, physically *starving*. There is work to be done. I want Christians to see that it is time to step outside the walls of their sanctuaries and start doing the work of ministry.

Ministry is work. I know to some Christians work is a curse word. But what we believe has to extend past Sunday morning, and we have to get our hands dirty. I remember doing a food distribution on a Tuesday in a church parking lot. As I walked past the line, I had a person stop me before we even started and say, "Pastor, I know you pray, because last time you prayed for my feet, and now they are fine. But now I've got a lump, and I need you to pray with me about my lump. I need you to pray for my brother cause he just went into the hospital." That is God. These people know they are going to get some food, but they also know that we will pray with them. That is what the Church should be.

I have found success in this formula: commitment leads to consistency, which leads to credibility, which leads to an open heart to receive, which leads to impact.

1 Thessalonians 5:4-15   But you, brethren, are not in darkness, so that this Day should overtake you as a thief. 5 You are all sons of light and sons of the day. We are not of the night nor of darkness. 6 Therefore let us not sleep, as others do, but let us watch and be sober. 7 For those who sleep, sleep at night, and those who get drunk are drunk at night. 8 But let us who are of the day be sober, putting on the breastplate of faith and love, and as a helmet the hope of salvation. 9 For God did not appoint us to wrath, but to obtain salvation through our Lord Jesus Christ, 10 who died for us, that whether we wake or sleep, we should live together with Him. 11 Therefore comfort each other and edify one another, just as you also are doing. 12 And we urge you, brethren, to recognize those who labor among you, and are over you in the Lord and admonish you, 13 and to esteem them very highly in love for their work's sake. Be at peace among yourselves.

14 Now we exhort you, brethren, warn those who are unruly, comfort the fainthearted, uphold the weak, be patient with all. 15 See that no one renders evil for evil to anyone, but always pursue what is good both for yourselves and for all.

This is who we are. We are sons of the light and sons of the day. The passage goes on to explain what it looks like for us to live as sons of the light. It's not just about what we don't do; it's a lot more about what we *do*.

Our comfort is not found in sleeping or resting, but in edifying and serving one another. When we provide a family with a meal they wouldn't have had otherwise, they are comforted in that moment. I remember taking a box of food to a shut-in, a woman in her eighties who could not physically leave her house for groceries. When we pulled up to her house, she had just eaten her last meal that day and had absolutely no food left. What a joy for both of us to experience God's provision. On another occasion we called a food pantry, and they said that they were closing early that day because they were out of food. We headed there with our truck full of food, and the guy's eyes lit up as he said, "God is so faithful. We were out of food." That is being a light. It is not necessarily anything special; it is just recognizing we can be a light in a dark place. It is comforting and edifying someone else by doing something for them.

Paul uses strong language here. He *admonishes* us. He *exhorts* us. This call to "comfort the fainthearted, uphold the weak, be patient with all" is not just a suggestion. It is *who we are* as we live in the light.

The light bulb is an incredible invention which drastically changed the way people live. But there are some things we must do to maintain our light, because a surge of power into a light bulb can make it explode and burn out. This happens with Christians. We get a surge of energy and passion in our lives, we run and run, and then we burn out and fade away. If we are going to exhort people, to encourage people, and to live showing our good works as an example to others, we must pace ourselves for our good works to continue and not fade away.

There are five things we need to do in order to maintain our light, and to serve with balance in a way that is sustainable for the long haul.

Be Prepared

The first thing we need to do is be prepared. We need to dress appropriately. I'm not talking about what clothes we wear to church. 1 Thessalonians tells us to put on the breastplate of faith and the helmet of salvation. But in Ephesians, Paul says to put on the breastplate of *righteousness* and the shield of faith. It is likely that Paul was just using the symbolism interchangeably. But it is also worth considering this: how are you made righteous? You are saved by grace through faith. So really your breastplate of righteousness is just a byproduct of your faith. Why do you put on a breastplate? Paul says the shield of faith is to quench the fiery darts of the enemy—so something doesn't pierce your chest and reach your heart. So when we have the breastplate of righteousness in Ephesians and the breastplate of faith in Thessalonians, we are talking about essentially the same thing. The bottom line is that we have new qualities to put on. If you want to have a light you need to learn how to dress appropriately. Put on a helmet of salvation. Learn how to guard your heart by faith and by righteousness. Because if you don't learn how to dress appropriately, you are going to fall to the wind and to the whims of false doctrines. And it is going to harm your ministry.

Be Sober

The next word is one we hear often: sober. Being sober means being self-controlled; it means to keep your wits about you. We need to be sober when life happens. Growing up I would hear the word *sober* often in our family because my dad was a heavy drinker. When I was a kid, we had a quarter-barrel tap in a refrigerator in our basement. The adults didn't want to walk down the stairs, so guess who went to tap the beers for them? The kids. So at nine or ten years old, we did what anyone else would do in that situation: pour a little drink for yourself. All the examples we looked up to were drinking, and we followed suit. So I grew up hearing the word *sober* a lot—not seeing sober a lot, but hearing the word often. And I saw the effects of drunkenness and how it can affect a person's decision making.

Did you know that you can get drunk on other things besides alcohol? You can get drunk with power. You can get drunk with depression. You can get drunk with a lot of things. We need to learn how to be sober in all things. Self-control means balance. It means knowing when to stop. But it also means pressing on when things get tough.

Recently Elaine and I started exercising and taking some steps toward being healthier. I like to run, and I especially like to run outside. After I work out and do my weight lifting, I will go run a few miles. You learn a couple things when you do that. When you do a weight routine that takes about 50 minutes, doing push-ups and sit-ups and lifting weights, you burn a lot of energy. So if I go out and run without doing that, my run is much easier because I have not burned off a lot of energy. But if you go to run after you have exercised, you really have to learn to be self-controlled—especially when you run outside.

Running outside is much different than running on a treadmill, because a treadmill is a controlled environment. When you run outside, you deal with wind and hills and all kinds of things that impede your progress. The key is being temperate enough to understand that when you turn your back and come down the other direction, that same wind that now feels like it is hindering me is going to be pushing me forward. So whether the wind is in my face or the blessing of God's wind is pushing behind me, I still have to learn to be temperate. When the wind is at my back, I still don't want to run too fast, because I end up exerting too much energy, and then I don't have enough energy to finish the race.

So even in the moments of blessing in your life, learn to be self-controlled and sober in the refreshing seasons just as you do in the seasons of calamity.

Be Vigilant

Be vigilant. Keep awake. Watch. Your adversary the devil walks about like a roaring lion, seeking whom he may devour. When lions hunt they tend to seek animals who have pulled away from the herd. They look for the ones that are young, newly born, or lacking the strength to fend for themselves. If our enemy is like this, we need to stay vigilant. We need to keep watch for each other.

I've had the privilege of leading many mission trips over the years. At one point, my friends Kevin and Anne lived in England, and we led a group of forty teenagers on a trip there. My head was on a swivel the whole time because I was constantly making sure I knew where everyone was. Every parent knows what this is like. When you take your child to a crowded place, you are always on guard. This is being vigilant. We need to do the same thing with our spiritual lives. We need to be watchful so that something is not trying to put out our light. We have an enemy who wants to pick us off from the herd.

Be Humble

We are also called to be humble. In Romans 12:3 Paul tells us not to think of ourselves more highly than we ought. When you lose your humility and start thinking of yourself more highly then you should, pride will *always* throw you off balance. God gives grace to the humble. Jesus Christ humbled Himself to the point of death, and to death on the cross. Humility is one of the greatest assets to living a life of balance.

I was coming back from St. Louis, and I was in a Taco Bell in Kentucky. There was a man sitting at a table, and I was standing in the line. I felt God tell me, "Go preach to him." It was eight o'clock at night, and I was tired. I had just driven up the day before, and I was driving back the next day. And I thought, "I don't know. I just don't want to talk to him. What if he is going to think I am weird because I am a Christian?" So, being the strong Christian that I am, I got my Taco Bell, went to my car, and never said a word. I have to repent for being prideful, for being too worried about my schedule, being too tired to bother. I do not always get it right. But the times I have gotten it right, it has meant laying down my own pride, my own schedule, and my own plans for God's. It is impossible to serve God without humility.

Be Peaceful

Lastly, we must be peaceful.

Romans 12:18 If it is possible, as much as depends on you, live peaceably with all men.

Jesus said in John 14:27, "My peace I give to you." Jesus has given us His peace. This reminds me of John 8:2–12 and the woman caught in adultery. This story is interesting because when the scribes and Pharisees bring this woman to Jesus, they are trying to trick Him. Typically when someone is trying to trick or catch us, our anxiety levels rise quickly. Why is that? It is because pride starts to enter in, and we start thinking, "Somebody is going to make me look like a fool!" And that is a form of pride, because we are worried about what people are going to think of us.

When they bring the adulterous woman before Jesus, there are a few issues at play. First of all in order to commit adultery, she was most likely betrothed to someone, and according to law, they should have brought the man too. They would have stoned both of them, not just her. The motive was not justice, but deception. Jesus brings instant peace to this moment. Can you imagine the anxiety in this woman, about to be stoned to death, and filled with shame as she stands condemned before her community? I don't picture a peaceful moment here.

The religious leaders challenge Jesus: "What are we going to do? Shouldn't we stone her?" Jesus simply bends down and begins to write on the ground. What a disarming action in a moment like this. This must have dropped some of the tension and shifted the mood to curiosity, as those watching probably thought, "What in the world is He doing?" Then He stands up and says, "Let him who is without sin cast the first stone." He doesn't walk around saying, "You are a bunch of hypocrites and liars. You are trying to trick me." He simply says, "Hey, whoever has not sinned, let him cast the first stone." What happens next? One by one they start dropping their stones and walking away. Jesus takes a volatile situation and diffuses it by bringing this peaceful countenance to the scene. Then He looks at the woman and asks, "Where are thy accusers?"

For many Christians in this same situation, the first thought would have been, "I am going to address this sinner here, because she has obviously committed adultery. Clearly she needs to be corrected." What does Jesus do? "Woman, where are thy accusers?" *There are none.* "Neither do I accuse you." What greater peace for someone to look at you in your sin and shame and say, "Neither do I accuse you. Go and sin no more"?

Another example of peace is found in the story of the centurion in Matthew 8. Jesus has just publicly healed a leper, so you can imagine the frenzy that has ensued. A centurion has a deathly ill servant. If you have ever been around someone who is dangerously ill, and you are trusting God with that person's life, you know that death tends to bring a sense of urgency. You pray like you have never prayed before. But often the thing missing in these situations is peace. So this Roman centurion, respected and feared in society, humbles himself and desperately asks Jesus for help. Jesus agrees to go, but the centurion, trusting Jesus' power, says, "You don't need to go. You can just speak a word. I am a man under authority and I have men under authority to me. I tell this one to go, and they go." Jesus stands back, astonished by the man's faith.

There is a real connection between peace and faith. Faith is tenacious; it is active; it is forceful; yet it carries great calm because it knows who is in control. So I look at the story of the centurion, and I think that what Jesus wanted to say was, "I have not seen such great peace in all of Israel. In the midst of this situation in which your servant is going to die, you are at such peace and such calm that you understand, 'Just speak a word and it will be done.'" Faith in Jesus brings peace in calamity.

Then, of course, there is the story of Jesus calming the storm. He is asleep in the bow of the boat. His disciples are panicking. What does He wake up and say? *Peace, be still.* How can we expect to be a light to the world if we get washed away by everything that happens to us? Some Christians are strobe lights, flashing on and off every time a trial hits. These people wear me out. They make my eyes burn. In the darkness and the storms, we need our light to keep shining. This brings peace in your own life and the lives of those around you. This means that if you encounter someone else who is facing a trial, you don't shy away. Do not dim your light in fear that it might offend someone. Jesus can calm the storm of your cancer, your financial ruin, your strained marriage. Do not shy away from that message. Speak that peace into the lives of others.

Remember these things. Be prepared. Dress appropriately. Don't come to the battle without armor. Be sober, self-controlled, keeping your mind and wits about you. Be vigilant, keep awake, watch. Be humble. Don't think of yourself more highly than you should. Be peaceful. Serving like Christ is a lifelong mission. It is a marathon, not a sprint. Stay balanced, because there is a lot left to do.

Philippians 4:6-7 Be anxious for nothing, but in everything by prayer and supplication, with thanksgiving, let your requests be made known to God; 7 and the peace of God, which surpasses all understanding, will guard your hearts and minds through Christ Jesus.

SERVING RELATIONALLY

1 Samuel 16:19-23 Therefore Saul sent messengers to Jesse, and said, "Send me your son David, who is with the sheep." 20 And Jesse took a donkey loaded with bread, a skin of wine, and a young goat, and sent them by his son David to Saul. 21 So David came to Saul and stood before him. And he loved him greatly, and he became his armor bearer. 22 Then Saul sent to Jesse, saying, "Please let David stand before me, for he has found favor in my sight." 23 And so it was, whenever the spirit from God was upon Saul, that David would take a harp and play it with His hand. Then Saul would become refreshed and well, and the distressing spirit would depart from him.

At first this might not seem important. A young man named David knows how to play the harp, so he is invited to play for Saul, the king. The backstory is that Israel wants to be like the other nations, so they demand God give them a king. God lets them choose, and they pick Saul, who is tall and good-looking. Saul makes some poor decisions as king, which leads in part to this troubling spirit he experiences. But when David comes and plays the harp, Saul feels at rest. Saul is so pleased that he even makes David his armor bearer. David is simply a young man, called upon to serve the king. But if we skip back a few verses, we can see the significance of David's service.

1 Samuel 16:1, 6-13 Now the Lord said to Samuel, "How long will you mourn for Saul, seeing I have rejected him from reigning over Israel? Fill your horn with oil, and go; I am sending you to Jesse the Bethlehemite. For I have provided Myself a king among his sons."

6 So it was, when they came, that he looked at Eliab and said, "Surely the Lord's anointed is before Him!" 7 But the Lord said to Samuel, "Do not look at his appearance or at his physical stature, because I have refused him. For the Lord does not see as man sees; for man looks at the outward appearance, but the Lord looks at the heart."

Service is about the heart, not ability.

8 So Jesse called Abinadab, and made him pass before Samuel. And he said, "Neither has the Lord chosen this one." 9 Then Jesse made Shammah pass by. And he said, "Neither has the Lord chosen this one." 10 Thus Jesse made seven of his sons pass before Samuel. 11 And Samuel said to Jesse, "The Lord has not chosen these." And Samuel said to Jesse, "Are all the young men here?" Then he said, "There remains yet the youngest, and there he is, keeping the sheep." And Samuel said to Jesse, "Send and bring him. For we will not sit down till he comes here." 12 So he sent and brought him in. Now he was ruddy, with bright eyes, and good-looking. And the Lord said, "Arise, anoint him; for this is the one!" 13 Then Samuel took the horn of oil and anointed him in the midst of his brothers; and the Spirit of the Lord came upon David from that day forward. So Samuel arose and went to Ramah.

The Lord comes to Samuel and asks him, "How long are you going to mourn the fact that Saul has failed as king? I have a king that I want for my people. And that king is David." This changes the whole perspective of what we just read. David is not just any young man; he has been anointed to become king. A young man who has been anointed to become king is serving the current king. Here we see David's character of humility.

1 Samuel 18:5-12   So David went out wherever Saul sent him, and behaved wisely. And Saul set him over the men of war, and he was accepted in the sight of all the people and also in the sight of Saul's servants. 6 Now it had happened as they were coming home, when David was returning from the slaughter of the Philistine, that the women had come out of all the cities of Israel, singing and dancing, to meet King Saul, with tambourines, with joy, and with musical instruments. 7 So the women sang as they danced, and said: "Saul has slain his thousands, And David his ten thousands." 8 Then Saul was very angry, and the saying displeased him; and he said, "They have ascribed to David ten thousands, and to me they have ascribed only thousands. Now what more can he have but the kingdom?" 9 So Saul eyed David from that day forward. 10 And it happened on the next day that the distressing spirit from God came upon Saul, and he prophesied inside the house. So David played music with his hand, as at other times; but there was a spear in Saul's hand. 11 And Saul cast the spear, for he said, "I will pin David to the wall!" But David escaped his presence twice. 12 Now Saul was afraid of David, because the Lord was with him, but had departed from Saul.

David is simply minding his own business, doing what God had called him to do. He has gained public fame for killing the

Philistine giant, Goliath, but he still serves the king by playing the harp—a mighty warrior who is not too proud to play music to calm down the king. That is humility. But when the people start to recognize and cheer for David, Saul becomes angry because he sees God's favor on David. So one day when David is playing his harp, Saul throws a spear at him, trying to kill him.

At this point, I would probably be handing in my letter of resignation as harpist. But David sticks around. David does not give up. Even though Saul has vowed to kill him, David keeps coming back to serve the king. **Service will always require sacrifice.** And even if you serve humbly and faithfully, that does not mean that your service will always be rewarded or even appreciated. But we read that God had his hand on David's life. I believe that if you serve humbly with a heart for God, His hand will be on your life.

> *1 Samuel 19:2-4 So Jonathan told David, saying, "My father Saul seeks to kill you. Therefore please be on your guard until morning, and stay in a secret place and hide. 3 And I will go out and stand beside my father in the field where you are, and I will speak with my father about you. Then what I observe, I will tell you." 4 Thus Jonathan spoke well of David to Saul his father, and said to him, "Let not the king sin against his servant, against David, because he has not sinned against you, and because his works have been very good toward you.*

Jonathan selflessly taking a stand for his friend is another example of service. He literally stands in the gap between his father and his friend, putting his own life on the line.

> *1 Samuel 18:1-5 Now when he had finished speaking to Saul, the soul of Jonathan was knit to the soul of David,*

and Jonathan loved him as his own soul. 2 Saul took him that day, and would not let him go home to his father's house anymore. 3 Then Jonathan and David made a covenant, because he loved him as his own soul. 4 And Jonathan took off the robe that was on him and gave it to David, with his armor, even to his sword and his bow and his belt. 5 So David went out wherever Saul sent him, and behaved wisely. And Saul set him over the men of war, and he was accepted in the sight of all the people and also in the sight of Saul's servants.

Jonathan's soul is knit to David's. This is the type of intimate friendship that comes when we are willing to serve one another. Jonathan removes his robe and gives it to David. He takes off his armor, his sword, his bow, his belt, and he gives them to David. This act might seem insignificant, but it symbolizes something of immense significance. Since Jonathan is the son of the king, he would be next in line for the throne. But Jonathan recognizes God's hand on David, and he has the courage to lay down his rightful inheritance and hand it over to his friend. That is what this transaction symbolizes. His heart to serve is such that he is willing to lay down his own agenda to serve David. He literally gives up everything he has. That is true servanthood.

1 Samuel 20:1-4 Then David fled from Naioth in Ramah, and went and said to Jonathan, "What have I done? What is my iniquity, and what is my sin before your father, that he seeks my life?" 2 So Jonathan said to him, "By no means! You shall not die! Indeed, my father will do nothing either great or small without first telling me. And why should my father hide this thing from me? It is not so!" 3 Then David took an oath again, and said, "Your father certainly knows that I have found favor in your eyes, and he has said, 'Do not let Jonathan know this, lest he be grieved.' But truly, as the Lord lives and as your soul lives, there is but a step between me and death." 4 So Jonathan said to David, "Whatever you yourself desire, I will do it for you."

Next, Jonathan made a pact with David to protect him from Saul. Essentially, his actions said, "I am willing to go as far as I must—even to death—in order to protect my friend." Jonathan makes good on that promise, dying in battle on David's behalf, leaving behind a disabled son named Mephibosheth. And David takes in Mephibosheth because of his oath to his friend Jonathan. David could have easily blown off this oath, which was made in private between David and Jonathan. But David honors his friend through this incredible act of service, to take in his friend's disabled son as his own. I believe that he does so in part because of Jonathan's faithful service to him. That is the effect servanthood has on others. That is the result of a life committed to service.

I will be honest with you, serving is not easy. Serving has a lot of challenges. It sounds great, and when we serve people in our community, most people are really grateful. Most people are thankful, but some aren't. Some people are angry or dissatisfied or ungrateful. That can make service challenging. Nobody has threatened us, but it could happen, just like David experiences in this story.

1 Samuel 24:1-7 Now it happened, when Saul had returned from following the Philistines, that it was told him, saying, "Take note! David is in the Wilderness of En Gedi." 2 Then Saul took three thousand chosen men from all Israel, and went to seek David and his men on the Rocks of the Wild Goats. 3 So he came to the sheepfolds by the road, where there was a cave; and Saul went in to attend to his needs. (David and his men were staying in the recesses of the cave.) 4 Then the men of David said to him, "This is the day of which the Lord said to you, 'Behold, I will deliver your enemy into your hand, that you may do to him as it seems good to you.'" And David arose and secretly cut off a corner of Saul's robe. 5 Now it happened afterward that David's heart troubled him because he had cut Saul's robe. 6 And he said to his men, "The Lord forbid that I should do this thing to my master, the Lord's anointed, to stretch out my hand against him, seeing he is the anointed of the Lord." 7 So David restrained his servants with these words, and did not allow them to rise against Saul. And Saul got up from the cave and went on his way.

Saul is serious about hunting down David, so much so that he brings 3,000 men. They go to the exact cave where David and his servants are hiding, giving David the opportunity to kill Saul. David's men tell him, "God has delivered him into your hands. Let's kill him!" But David, in his humility, simply cuts off a corner of Saul's robe, and then begins to repent for what he has done. He believes so strongly in God's plan that he feels wrong for opposing the king God has put in place. This does not just happen once; it happens again in chapter 26.

1 Samuel 26:5-10 So David arose and came to the place where Saul had encamped. And David saw the place where Saul lay, and Abner the son of Ner, the commander of his army. Now Saul lay within the camp, with the people encamped all around him. 6 Then David answered, and said to Ahimelech the Hittite and to Abishai the son of Zeruiah, brother of Joab, saying, "Who will go down with me to Saul in the camp?" And Abishai said, "I will go down with you." 7 So David and Abishai came to the people by night; and there Saul lay sleeping within the camp, with his spear stuck in the ground by his head. And Abner and the people lay all around him. 8 Then Abishai said to David, "God has delivered your enemy into your hand this day. Now therefore, please, let me strike him at once with the spear, right to the earth; and I will not have to strike him a second time!" 9 But David said to Abishai, "Do not destroy him; for who can stretch out His hand against the Lord's anointed, and be guiltless?" 10 David said furthermore, "As the Lord lives, the Lord shall strike him, or his day shall come to die, or he shall go out to battle and perish."

Now a man very loyal to David, Abishai, offers, "Let me do it. I won't miss, he will be dead, and this whole thing will be over. You've got a right, let's end this thing right now." But David states that Saul is in God's hands and therefore he must honor him. Service is about honoring people. Service involves laying down your rights. And here is David honoring Saul because of the gift and the status and the platform that God has laid upon Saul. I love that, because I believe that the true test of service comes when you don't agree with the person you are serving. That is hard service. Our calling is not to serve begrudgingly, but to serve with the heart of David, saying "I have no right to lay my hand on him." So even though David truly does have every right to lay his hand on Saul, he surrenders that right as a true servant.

Despite all of David's flaws, he has some extraordinary qualities—which is probably why he is called a man after God's own heart in 1 Samuel 13:14 and in Acts 13:22. Perhaps the most notable flaw that comes to mind would be David's situation with Bathsheba.

The story goes that David sends everybody out to war, and though he should accompany them, he stays behind. During this idle time, he catches a glimpse of Bathsheba bathing on her roof, and he brings her to his palace and sleeps with her. This sets into motion a series of attempts to cover up David's sin, culminating in sending Bathsheba's husband into battle to die. Now David is an adulterer and a murderer, yet God calls him a man after His own heart. Clearly David was not perfect; that is not what God is asking of us. But he does desire a heart to serve, and that is what set David apart.

Ruth's Service

We have seen these great stories about David serving Saul and Jonathon serving David, but the book of Ruth contains another great story about service. The story begins with an Israelite woman and her husband in the midst of a famine in their land. Naomi and her husband decide to move to Moab to seek food. Nowhere are they commanded by God to go; they make this decision on their own. So Naomi and her husband move to Moab and their two sons marry two Moabite women, one of whom is named Ruth. But seemingly not long after, Naomi's husband dies, followed by her two sons. Naomi is left stranded in Moab with her two daughters-in-law.

One of the defining moments in the story comes when Naomi tells her two daughters-in-law, "There is nothing left for me here, so I am leaving, and you need to go on with your lives." They weep and cry, and one of the young women says, "You're right," and moves on. But Ruth stops, looks at Naomi, and says, "You know what? I am not leaving you." That is the heart of a servant. Naomi is not her mother—she is her mother-in-law—but Ruth promises not to leave her side, not to take the easy way out and abandon her.

Out of Ruth's decision to serve, an amazing story unfolds. Ruth begins to glean. She goes to a field and follows after the workers, picking up the excess scraps to take home to Naomi, an activity encouraged by Jewish law as a way to help the poor. As if by chance, the field from which she gleans is owned by a man named Boaz, a relative of Naomi's.

Boaz is a wealthy man, very well known and very successful. Ruth finds favor with Boaz, and he allows her special privileges in his field. Naomi sees the promise in Boaz's favor, and she instructs Ruth to seek out Boaz alone in the place where he would be sleeping. Boaz wakes up one morning, and here is Ruth, curled up around his feet sleeping. That is all. But Boaz sees something in Ruth at that moment. He sees her humility, her boldness, and her servant's heart. He knows the story of her loyalty to Naomi, and she obtains favor in his eyes.

Serving brings favor. Boaz, as you might know from the story, ends up marrying Ruth. But the epilogue to the story contains an incredible turn of history. After Boaz and Ruth are married, Ruth has a son name Obed. If you know your genealogy, you know that "Obed begot Jesse, and Jesse begot David." So David's great grandmother is Ruth.

So perhaps David's heart of servanthood can be credited in part to his great grandmother. And she was a gentile woman. Not from a Jew, not from the lineage, not from the great nation of Israel, but a widowed gentile woman whom God redeems for His purpose. Do you think that Ruth knew in the moment that she decided to serve her mother-in-law or humbly glean in a field that it would lead her to become part of the line of the king of Israel, David? And we know that the line of David eventually leads to the Messiah, Jesus. What a testimony from one bold act of service.

Christ's Service

Matthew 20:28   Just as the Son of Man did not come to be served, but to serve, and to give His life a ransom for many.

So Jesus did not come to be served but to serve, and that is the base scripture.

So here we have Jesus: "I did not come to be served, but to serve." And that is why I believe that God looked at David and said, "A man after my own heart."

Matthew 26:52-54 But Jesus said to him, "Put your sword in its place, for all who take the sword will perish by the sword. 53 Or do you think that I cannot now pray to My Father, and He will provide Me with more than twelve legions of angels? 54 How then could the Scriptures be fulfilled, that it must happen thus?"

Here is Jesus in the garden just before His arrest. Peter pulls his sword and takes the ear of one of the soldiers. And Jesus tells him, "Put your sword away." He says, "Don't you think I could call a thousand angels?" There is a heart of a servant. Why? Because He came not to be served but to serve, and His service was to die for humanity.

Service requires a willing heart. Service is not a begrudging spirit. It is a willingness to do what is required and to obey God. Service is meant to honor and glorify God, not to bring glory to ourselves.

John 19:10-11 Then Pilate said to Him, "Are You not speaking to me? Do You not know that I have power to crucify You, and power to release You?" 11 Jesus answered, "You could have no power at all against Me unless it had been given you from above. Therefore the one who delivered Me to you has the greater sin."

Christ's sacrifice is voluntary. No one has forced His hand. He tells Pilate that He answers to a higher power; this is a path He has chosen, not one forced upon Him.

I would love to say that this is the attitude that I have in my life at all times. When I first gave my heart to Jesus, I decided that I wanted to serve in the youth ministry. I approached the youth pastor and told him that I felt like I was supposed to be involved. Any youth pastor loves to hear that another adult wants to serve and contribute to the ministry. Eventually I got pretty involved and was giving a lot of my time to the ministry.

There came a time when the youth pastor had a position open up, basically as his right-hand man. Another guy who had been serving in the ministry was also in consideration for the position. In my immature understanding of service, I remember telling Elaine that obviously I was the man for the job. I knew God had specifically called me to this ministry, so I knew He would give me this position. It wasn't that the other guy was a bad choice. But I knew this was what God called me to, so obviously, I thought, God wants to promote me.

Long story short, it did not end up that way. I got passed over and the other guy became the right-hand man. Now I had a decision to make. I could have just packed it up and said, "All right, I am done. Obviously this youth pastor is a knucklehead and he can't see the gift in me." But I believe that God was trying to teach me something.

We stick around and serve because it is not about us; it is about Him. And I had to learn a valuable lesson that whether I am passed over or chosen, I am here to serve and to glorify and honor God.

SERVING IN MARRIAGE

This chapter is all about serving in marriage. If you are not married, do not skip over this part, because you may be married someday, and the principle of service in marriage can help to inform all other relationships in your life, especially with the opposite sex. Even single Christians should have an informed view of marriage. The primary concern of this chapter is service; once again rooted in Matthew 20:28, where Jesus says, "I didn't come to be served; I came to serve." If our marriages are to reflect Jesus, they must be founded on service.

Ephesians 5:1-2 Therefore be imitators of God as dear children. 2 And walk in love, as Christ also has loved us and given Himself for us, an offering and a sacrifice to God for a sweet-smelling aroma.

The command in this verse is for everyone: be imitators of God. In the preceding passage Paul talks about letting no corrupt words come out of your mouth, letting all bitterness, wrath, and anger be taken away from you, being kind to one another, tender-hearted, forgiving one another even as God in

Christ forgave you. Then comes this verse, ushered in by the word *therefore*. What are we to do instead of speaking harshly and bitterly to one another? Forgive. How? Imitate God. He has called you dear children, and He has loved and forgiven you so that you may walk in love.

> *John 13:34-35   A new commandment I give to you, that you love one another; as I have loved you, that you also love one another. 35 By this all will know that you are My disciples, if you have love for one another.*

It is impossible to follow Jesus without loving others. That is the mark of a disciple. The concept of love here is deeper than what we ordinarily think. As a teenager, "love" was such an easy word to throw around. "I am in love, I love you!" we tell our high school sweethearts, and it sounds so cute and special. But as adults we see that what we thought was so deep was actually so shallow. In reality, even as adults our concept of love is lacking.

As Christians, we need a deeper definition of love. Imitators of God. God so loved the world that He gave His only begotten Son. Those of us who have children can grasp the severity of this statement: a love that would cause one to give up a child. Now think about doing that for people who may not care or love you back. That's heavy. That is love. That is crazy love. I love my kids so much I would protect them from anything. But God loved us so much that He took all the protection off of Jesus and had Him become sin, which separated Him from His father. When you think about love in that way, the tingly feeling you get when you see your sweetheart begins to pale in comparison.

> *John 15:12-13   This is My commandment, that you love one another as I have loved you. 13 Greater love has no one than this, than to lay down one's life for his friends.*

God's definition of love is not like ours. It is deeper and more costly. It is self-sacrificial. That is ultimate servanthood.

Spirit-Led Marriage

Ephesians 5:15-33 See then that you walk circumspectly, not as fools but as wise, 16 redeeming the time, because the days are evil. 17 Therefore do not be unwise, but understand what the will of the Lord is. 18 And do not be drunk with wine, in which is dissipation; but be filled with the Spirit, 19 speaking to one another in psalms and hymns and spiritual songs, singing and making melody in your heart to the Lord, 20 giving thanks always for all things to God the Father in the name of our Lord Jesus Christ, 21 submitting to one another in the fear of God. 22 Wives, submit to your own husbands, as to the Lord. 23 For the husband is head of the wife, as also Christ is head of the church; and He is the Savior of the body. 24 Therefore, just as the church is subject to Christ, so let the wives be to their own husbands in everything. 25 Husbands, love your wives, just as Christ also loved the church and gave Himself for her, 26 that He might sanctify and cleanse her with the washing of water by the word, 27 that He might present her to Himself a glorious church, not having spot or wrinkle or any such thing, but that she should be holy and without blemish. 28 So husbands ought to love their own wives as their own bodies; he who loves his wife loves himself. 29 For no one ever hated his own flesh, but nourishes and cherishes it, just as the Lord does the church. 30 For we are members of His body, of His flesh and of His bones. 31 "For this reason a man shall leave his father and mother and be joined to his wife, and the two shall become one flesh." 32 This is a great mystery, but I speak concerning Christ and the church. 33 Nevertheless let each one of you in particular so love his own wife as himself, and let the wife see that she respects her husband.

15 See then that you walk circumspectly, not as fools but as wise, 16 redeeming the time, because the days are evil. 17 Therefore do not be unwise, but understand what the will of the Lord is.

"Circumspectly" is a big word meaning cautiously and with sensitivity. "Redeeming the time" is such a profound thought, because one of the biggest dangers we face as Christians is letting the days slip away from us and missing chances for obedience to God. Time is a precious commodity. It is a non-renewable resource.

Sometimes we wish there were more hours in the day, but the truth is that if you can't figure how to deal with the 24 hours you get, more hours in a day would just mean more opportunity to waste the time you have been given.

We don't need more time; we need more wisdom. If we are going to be imitators of God, then we need to line up our priorities with His.

18 And do not be drunk with wine, in which is dissipation; but be filled with the Spirit.

Verse 18 instructs us not to be drunk with wine but to be filled with the Spirit. This verse is key to the entire passage.

The best example I have for this verse comes from my own life, and it is extremely personal to me. Growing up with a father who was an alcoholic, I have seen firsthand the effects drunkenness has. I have seen what it brings out in a person. In the old days, liquor was commonly called spirits. So when Jesus is saying do not be drunk, He is saying, "Do not engage that spirit, but be filled with the Spirit, the Holy Spirit."

In the same way that being filled with spirits (drunkenness) affects your judgment, your thoughts, your actions, your communication, being filled with the Spirit is even more powerful. The Holy Spirit can change your judgments, your thoughts, your actions, and your communication in marriage to make you an imitator of God. Without the Holy Spirit, you will not have a good marriage. James writes, "Faith without works is dead." Serving without the Holy Spirit is also dead. You do not have it within yourself to accurately imitate God without His Spirit inside you working through you.

The Holy Spirit is the most misunderstood and neglected person of the trinity. Yet the Holy Spirit is vital to the Christian life, and apart from the Holy Spirit it is impossible for us to rightly know the other members of the trinity. Jesus tells His disciples it is better for Him to leave them, because when He leaves He will send a Helper in His place. If Jesus, the Son of God, performer of miracles, slain on our behalf and risen from the dead, says that it is better that He leave so that the Holy Spirit can come, then we should probably pay attention to the Holy Spirit.

The Holy Spirit came to convict the world of sin. He came to lead us and guide us into all truth. Those who are led by the Spirit of God are the sons of God. These are all things the scriptures tell us about the Holy Spirit. These are crucial truths.

If you want to be a husband who leads and protects his family, then you have to know how to hear the voice of God in the Holy Spirit. Those who are the sons of God are led by the Spirit of God. If you want to be a wife who knows how to respect and honor her husband, then you have to know how to hear the voice of God in the Holy Spirit. Because there will be times as a husband when you will not know all of the answers, God has given you a Helper. There will be times as a wife when your husband does not deserve your respect, but the Bible doesn't just say to respect him when he deserves it. You will need a Helper. The Holy Spirit is the Helper God has sent us.

> *19 speaking to one another in psalms and hymns and spiritual songs, singing and making melody in your heart to the Lord, 20 giving thanks always for all things to God the Father in the name of our Lord Jesus Christ.*

Some of our biggest problems in marriage come in speaking to one another. Communication is hard. God's Word tells married couples here to speak to one another in psalms and hymns and spiritual songs. I don't sing to my wife because she would probably leave me. I have been told I have a voice that can clear a room—that is not a compliment. But I can speak to my wife in psalms and hymns and spiritual songs. Because psalms and hymns are all about giving thanks to God, crying out to God, relying on God. Our communication should always point one another to that.

Later, the text talks about husbands washing their wives in the water of the Word. Water represents the Holy Spirit. So husbands, don't just speak God's Word to your wife, let the Holy Spirit teach you both through His word. This passage is about marriage, but it is also all about the Holy Spirit.

When you learn to wash your wife with the water of the Word and speak in psalms and hymns, you will find that some of the psalms are dark and difficult. But the Holy Spirit wants to lead your marriage through those dark places. Often in the psalms, David is faced with his own sin. He is humbled and brought to repentance. The Holy Spirit wants to do that in your marriage.

Mutual Submission

> *21 submitting to one another in the fear of God*

In our modern day, we shy away from this verse. We associate submission with oppression. But this verse says we should submit one to another. This is a mutual submission—give and take. I missed this concept in my marriage for a long time. My wife is very submissive, and she served me better than I deserved, but I didn't understand mutual submission.

Sometimes I ask wives, "How many children do you have?" And they may say one, two, three, four. I tell them to add one to that because your husband is your other child. Sadly, this is too common and too true. Men act like grown boys, and their wives are forced to pick up the slack.

It can be fun and cute to joke about being a grown boy, but there comes a time for a man to be a man. A man takes responsibility. He takes a responsibility for his wife. He takes responsibility for his children. A man praises and encourages his wife. We need to apologize to our wives where we have failed, because I promise we have failed. A man does not find his identity in his job or his ability to provide. Your identity is found in Christ.

Now I am going to talk to the wives a little bit.

Wives, you have to learn to build your husbands up. Gary Chapman has written a book called *The Five Love Languages;* I believe an overwhelming percentage of men, if they read this book, will find that the primary way that they feel loved is through words of affirmation. Men need to be affirmed. We live in a competitive society that is constantly concerned with who is better than who. Men need affirmation, and the one person they really need it from is their wife.

Proverbs 14:1 The wise woman builds her house, but the foolish pulls it down with her hands.

Often the way the foolish woman pulls down her house is with her words. Your husband does not need to constantly hear the ways he has failed or fallen short. He likely already knows those things. Many times men already feel like dirt bags; they don't need your reminders. You might be right, but the price you are paying for being right is more than you know.

Sometimes it isn't worth being right, because the price you are paying is destroying your leader. And then you want to look at him and say, "Why aren't you leading?" Calling your husband a failure may be telling the truth, but it can also be a self-fulfilling prophecy. You will speak identity into the people closest to you. A wise woman uses her words to build up her house—especially the leader and head of the household.

This doesn't take men off the hook. We need to understand that we lead our wives in such a way that we lay our lives down for them. If it sounds hard for wives to submit, how about the command for husbands to lay down their lives? It is literally a call to die. Now submission doesn't sound so bad.

Wives, even when your husbands are knuckleheads, you have to find a way to encourage them, to believe in them, to speak life into them. You are the greatest voice to that man next to God, and there will be times when your husband will be hiding from God, but it is much harder for him to hide from you.

22 Wives, submit to your own husbands, as to the Lord. 23 For the husband is head of the wife, as also Christ is head of the church; and He is the Savior of the body. 24 Therefore, just as the church is subject to Christ, so let the wives be to their own husbands in everything.

Words are powerful. When Jesus meets the centurion, and the centurion tells Jesus his servant was sick, Jesus offers to go to the centurion's house and heal his servant. But the centurion says, "You don't even have to go. Just speak a word." This man is a military man, and he understands authority. He understands that Jesus has powers at His command that could heal His servant immediately.

This word *submission* is a military term here in Ephesians, just as it is in the story in Matthew. Different members of the armed forces have different ranks: sergeants, lieutenants, privates, etc. Sergeants have a saying, "Don't call me, 'sir;' I work for a living." This means that even though sergeants are in a position of authority, they are still enlisted men, not officers. They still go into battle with the troops, and they want the troops to understand, "I'm one of you." When you go into battle in your marriage, you need to remember that you are a unit. There is a chain of command, but when you are out on the battlefield, you are fighting for the same cause.

That is the way a husband and wife should be. We are not fighting against each other. We are fighting together against a common enemy. And understand that the devil wants nothing more than to destroy your marriage. Why do you think Solomon writes in Ecclesiastes 4:12, *And a threefold cord is not easily broken.* That should tell you that something or someone is trying to break that cord. Your threefold cord consists of husband, wife, and Jesus. The devil will use whatever it takes, be it a misunderstanding of submission, or a husband who makes himself impossible to respect and submit to, in order to break that cord.

Men, if you don't know how to lead, you are in luck. The Holy Spirit does. If God called you to make this woman your wife, then He has equipped you to lead her. If things are not going the way you had planned, and you want to know where the fault is, then go stand in front of a mirror and say, "God, I repent, and, Holy Spirit, I pray right now that you would invade my life and show me how to be the leader that you have called me to be."

Priorities

I tell people that God moved my family to Tennessee to start a church. Really God moved me to Tennessee to teach me how to be a better husband. It wasn't until we moved here that I really began to learn to honor and serve my wife. I'm still not there, but I am a whole lot closer than I was.

One practice I began was to give up five hours of work each week to spend with my wife. That is an hour per day. The only difference that five hours would make for my work was to boost my pride and ego. But that five hours with my wife could change my marriage, my children, and my ministry. Sometimes you just have to give up the overtime. Sometimes it just isn't worth it. Some days you need to take on some of your wife's tasks instead and just give her a chance to rest. Sometimes you simply need time together.

When we begin to humble ourselves and acknowledge God as our provider, there is no more pressure of feeling like the wheels will fall off the moment we rest. If you want to take a sick day one day, take a sick day to serve your wife. "Well, who's sick?" they ask. "My wife." "Well, what is she sick of?" "She is sick and tired of me being a jerk, so I am taking a sick day. I need to fix that sickness."

If your family is sick and struggling spiritually, no amount of work you do will ever prosper. If your work is the foundation of your identity as a man, then you are skewed in the wrong direction. That applies to business and ministry. I still need to be reminded of this truth.

Elaine normally has to get up around 4:30 in the morning to go to work. Recently I started waking up with her and making her breakfast while she gets ready. I am not patting myself on the back for this, because there was a long time when I did not do it. But this small act has totally changed the way she thinks about me, the way she reacts to me, and the way we communicate in our marriage.

Do I have to get up? No. But with all she does for me, I can get my lazy carcass out of bed to make breakfast. And it convicts me. Why didn't I learn to do this earlier? Why didn't I learn to serve her and honor her the way she deserves to be honored? I learn more every day.

The same thing that applies to the beginning of the day also applies to the end. Six o'clock at my house, you won't see me in front of a computer screen. You won't see me on my phone. It had better be an emergency if you see me on my phone after six o'clock. Whatever I did not get done that day can wait until tomorrow. It is not more important than my family. Once you realize this, it will change the way they think about you, the way they react to you, and the way your family communicates together.

Husbands, commit a day a week that you give to your wife. She deserves it. She deserves you. She didn't marry what you do for a living. She married you.

Wives, you did marry what he does for a living. I know you are thinking I just said the opposite. But although his career is not the foundation of his identity, it is a key part of how a man identifies himself. His career is a key part of how he serves and leads his family. He needs you to reinforce that, to encourage him, and to spur him on in that role. He needs to know that he is a good provider. He needs to know that you appreciate his getting up and going every day.

This is how you submit to one another.

Proverbs 31:28 says, *Her children and her husband will rise up and call her blessed.* We get hung up on Proverbs 31 because this woman is supposedly making all kinds of things with her bare hands, buying and selling goods and property, and somehow still has time for her family; she's everywhere, doing everything, all the time. I don't think Proverbs 31 is saying that a good wife has to do it all. I think it is saying what you do, wives, do it well. And the fact is that you are probably going to have to juggle a lot as a wife and a mother.

Husband, when you start to honor your wife, people around town will begin to look at you and think, "Dang, that dude's got it going on." People will start to notice that every week you go out on a date with your wife. They will think, "I wish I had that." You could. You just don't make your marriage that important. You might say your marriage is important, but faith without works is dead.

Faith without works is dead. Lip service means nothing to your wife. Trust me. Show her that you love her. Wash her in the water of the Word. Verse 29 says, *For no one ever hated his own flesh, but nourishes and cherishes it, just as the Lord does the church.* This means as much time, energy, and passion as you commit to your career or your hobbies or whatever it may be, you owe that same amount to your wife. Love her like you love your own body, your own self.

> *31 "For this reason a man shall leave his father and mother and be joined to his wife, and the two shall become one flesh." 32 This is a great mystery, but I speak concerning Christ and the church. 33 Nevertheless let each one of you in particular so love his own wife as himself, and let the wife see that she respects her husband.*

It was God's design and purpose that a man would leave his mother and father and be joined with a wife as one flesh. Genesis 2:18 tells us that God wanted to give man a helper. Not a servant—a helper. A helpmate.

Something I see happening too commonly is that a couple has a child, and the marriage immediately becomes secondary to the child. "But I've got a baby now, and that is my first responsibility!" You want to destroy your marriage? Put your baby before your spouse. You have to live with your spouse a whole lot longer than you are going to live with that child.

God has said to leave your mother and father and cleave unto your spouse—not cleave unto your children. But for many of us, that is what was modeled by our parents, and now we are modeling it to our children. Often the reason couples divorce after 25 or 30 years is because either a woman has devoted her life to her children and ignored her husband or a husband has devoted his life to his job and ignored his wife. When the kids are gone, they look at each other and say, "I don't know who you are."

Another thing I have seen happen is a man becoming jealous of his children. This may seem trivial, but when you live with someone day in and day out whom your wife constantly prioritizes over you, eventually that will take a toll. This is not to say that your children are not important. But you cannot properly love and parent your children if you are not properly loving and serving your spouse.

I love my kids, but they know you don't mess with date night. When Elaine and I spend time together, the children know that we have intentionally protected that time. And your children need to see that because one day when they are married, they will model what they have seen.

Marriage Is Service

I believe in marriage. I have not always been a good husband. I didn't have a good example of a husband in my dad. I am not blaming him, but I also know firsthand that what you model for your children is what they will learn. I also truly believe what Ephesians tells us about praying and being led by The Holy

Spirit—this is what enables me to lead my family as an imitator of God, loving my wife as Christ loved the Church.

We talked about how faith without works is dead, and serving without the Holy Spirit is dead. The Holy Spirit enables us to serve in the long haul of marriage without growing bitter or exhausted.

We talked about how husbands are called to wash our wives with the water of the Word. You can't do that without spending time in God's Word yourself. If you want to serve your wife, you have to be connected to the source. The Holy Spirit will speak to you and empower you through God's Word.

If you make a mistake, repent. The person who received the mistake, forgive. I'm not saying it will be easy, but understand that there is a real enemy, and it's not your spouse who wronged you. The devil is just looking for an opportunity to drive a wedge. The Bible says where there is strife, there is every form of evil work.

To repent is a sacrifice. To forgive is an act of service. Both are a laying down of self.

Don't allow strife into your marriage. Don't allow the sun to go down on your anger. Don't say, "We'll sleep on it." Stay up till two o'clock in the morning if that is what it takes to look each other in the eyes, repent, and forgive. Because if you let the problem fester and grow, it is going to be really ugly in the morning—much uglier than when it started.

But it is amazing how you will argue much less when you learn to submit to one another. Because when you start to submit to the Spirit of God you start to think, "I wonder what my spouse is thinking. How did he/she react to that? I wonder what his/her perspective is." That is called empathy and compassion. And when you start to do that, you also begin to think thoughts like, "Man, I probably didn't do that right. I probably didn't handle that right." That's called humility. And humility is one of the keys to service.

There is something to be said about physically serving your spouse. It teaches us something about who Jesus is. Jesus didn't just serve in word or in theory. No, He physically bore the cross. Carried it, went to it, was nailed to it. He lived His service. Find ways that you can physically and tangibly serve.

Jesus served in word as well as deed. Words matter. Words can tear others down. Jesus used words to build up. In His interaction with the woman caught in adultery, He could have easily and rightfully torn her apart with her words. After all, she is blatantly caught in sin, and He would not even be a hypocrite, because He has no sin. But Jesus takes a different approach. He invites any of those who are so quick to condemn her, if they are without sin, to cast the first stone. No takers. Everyone walks away, and He looks at her and says, "Go and sin no more."

When He speaks to the woman at the well, He asks about her husband. "I don't have a husband," she answers. "Ah, you speak well. You have had five and the one you are with now isn't your husband," He responds. But He does not condemn her. He doesn't call her a tramp or threaten to expose her. He offers her something better. He offers her living water. He offers her life.

There will be times in your life when your spouse will hurt you. Your spouse will wrong you. But I am telling you, if you hold that grudge, you might as well end your marriage now. Marriage has no place for unforgiveness. If you committed the wrong and you don't learn how to repent, then you might as well end your marriage now. Marriage has no place for stubborn pride.

If there is true repentance, then by golly there had better be true forgiveness. And if there is true forgiveness, then there had better by golly be true repentance! We have *all* sinned and fallen short of the glory of God.

You cannot serve in ministry if you are not willing to serve in marriage. You cannot serve your children if you are not willing to serve your spouse. God created marriage as a union of two imperfect people. He knew you would wrong each other. He knew you would have to repent and forgive. Repentance and forgiveness are acts of service to your spouse. Verbal encouragement and tangible help are acts of service to your spouse. Quality time and attention are acts of service to your spouse. Marriage is service. It is a picture of Christ and the Church, and we know that the Son of Man came not to be served, but to serve, and to give His life as a ransom for many.

CORPORATE SERVICE

Matthew 20:25-28 But Jesus called them to Himself and said, "You know that the rulers of the Gentiles lord it over them, and those who are great exercise authority over them. 26 Yet it shall not be so among you; but whoever desires to become great among you, let him be your servant. 27 And whoever desires to be first among you, let him be your slave— 28 just as the Son of Man did not come to be served, but to serve, and to give His life a ransom for many."

We have looked at this passage many times; verse 28 is the foundation for everything we have discussed. But there is more context to that powerful statement Jesus makes. The scene begins when the mother of James and John comes kneeling before Jesus with a request for Him: she wants her two sons to sit at His right and left hand in His kingdom.

The other ten disciples are upset, but what's a mom to do? A mom always wants the best for her kids, and what is better than to sit at the right and left hand of Jesus? But the ten are mad. I don't know if they are mad because their moms didn't think of it first—or maybe they are just wondering what is so special about James and John.

What strikes me in this passage is that I think they were expecting Jesus to rebuke them. In the church world, we act like wanting to be great is a sin. But Jesus does not rebuke them for wanting to be great. He says, "If you desire to be great, this is what you should do." We should desire to be great, as long as it is in humility with the first priority of glorifying God.

Numbers 32:5   Therefore they said, "If we have found favor in your sight, let this land be given to your servants as a possession. Do not take us over the Jordan."

Here, Israel is preparing to cross the Jordan into the promised land. A few of the tribes ask not to be taken across because they have cattle. My mom and her husband Gale live on about 40 acres and own about 40 head of cattle. I have asked Gale a lot of questions about the grass on their land, and that is a very important part of raising cattle. Pretty much all they do is eat grass all day. What a life.

So to me this does not seem like an unreasonable request. "We have cattle, this is good fertile land, and it's got grass, so this would be good for us. You can go ahead to the promised land, but we're just going to stay here."

Numbers 32:6-15   And Moses said to the children of Gad and to the children of Reuben: "Shall your brethren go to war while you sit here? 7 Now why will you discourage the heart of the children of Israel from going over into the land which the Lord has given them? 8 Thus your fathers did when I sent them away from Kadesh Barnea to see the land. 9 For when they went up to the Valley of Eshcol and saw the land, they discouraged the heart of the children of Israel, so that they did not go into the land which the Lord had given them. 10 So the Lord's anger was aroused on that day, and He swore an oath, saying, 11 'Surely none of the men who came up from Egypt, from twenty years old and above, shall see the land of which I swore to Abraham, Isaac, and Jacob, because they have not wholly followed Me, 12 except Caleb the son of Jephunneh, the Kenizzite, and Joshua the son of Nun, for they have wholly followed the Lord.' 13 So the Lord's anger was aroused against Israel, and He made them wander in the wilderness forty years, until all the generation that had done evil in the sight of the Lord was gone. 14 And look! You have risen in your fathers' place, a brood of sinful men, to increase still more the fierce anger of the Lord against Israel. 15 For if you turn away from following Him, He will once again leave them in the wilderness, and you will destroy all these people."

Wow. Obviously this is more serious than they thought. That is a strong rebuke. They are forbidden from entering the promised land simply because they wanted to take care of their cattle, their livelihood. What does this have to do with service? We are getting to that part.

Numbers 32:16-22 Then they came near to him and said: "We will build sheepfolds here for our livestock, and cities for our little ones, 17 but we ourselves will be armed, ready to go before the children of Israel until we have brought them to their place; and our little ones will dwell in the fortified cities because of the inhabitants of the land. 18 We will not return to our homes until every one of the children of Israel has received his inheritance. 19 For we will not inherit with them on the other side of the Jordan and beyond, because our inheritance has fallen to us on this eastern side of the Jordan."

> *20 Then Moses said to them: "If you do this thing, if you arm yourselves before the Lord for the war, 21 and all your armed men cross over the Jordan before the Lord until He has driven out His enemies from before Him, 22 and the land is subdued before the Lord, then afterward you may return and be blameless before the Lord and before Israel; and this land shall be your possession before the Lord."*

The tribes agree to leave their livestock behind and enter the land. Moses accepts, but he tells them that if they want to go, they are going to have to serve. They are going to have to put their own lives on hold and fight with the other tribes. This is what it looks like to wholly follow the Lord. Serving. To follow God, you have to be willing to put your own life and your own concerns aside and serve.

So these tribes build themselves a settlement, somewhere to keep their livestock and families, a place to feed the cattle and a place for their children to grow up. They set that up so that they can go to war with their brothers as God has instructed them.

This is a great picture for the Church in modern-day America. There is no doubt of our calling. We have not arrived because we have a beautiful facility that God has provided for us, and we are not finished just because we do a few food drives in the parking lot. We are called to serve other churches in order for them to win the land that God has for them. And then one day we will get to come back, not to this world, but to Heaven.

Serving is a corporate effort. Just as the tribes who wanted to stay behind were called to join their brothers and take the promised land, we are called to join with other churches in our communities to do God's work together.

How long do we have to keep doing this? Until Christ returns. We don't know when that will be, but we are called to keep serving until He comes back or takes us home. And when we die there will be another generation. They are going to raise up and they are going to take it. Our children and their children are going to carry on this legacy of service. So we must model faithful service before them as a body of believers. We are going to do this until the Lord comes back. Moses tells the tribes they will return when the work is done, and no sooner.

But our calling is not to go battle for the land across the Jordan—we have a different mission.

Matthew 25:34-40   Then the King will say to those on His right hand, 'Come, you blessed of My Father, inherit the kingdom prepared for you from the foundation of the world: 35 for I was hungry and you gave Me food; I was thirsty and you gave Me drink; I was a stranger and you took Me in; 36 I was naked and you clothed Me; I was sick and you visited Me; I was in prison and you came to Me.' 37 "Then the righteous will answer Him, saying, 'Lord, when did we see You hungry and feed You, or thirsty and give You drink? 38 When did we see You a stranger and take You in, or naked and clothe You? 39 Or when did we see You sick, or in prison, and come to You?' 40 And the King will answer and say to them, 'Assuredly, I say to you, inasmuch as you did it to one of the least of these My brethren, you did it to Me.'

This is our calling. This is our mission. Jesus came to seek and save that which is lost. We are called to follow His lead. You might say, "That's right, we need to seek and save that which is lost. So why are we helping churches? They are not lost." Not all the people we are called to serve are lost. They are Christians, but they still need us to serve them.

We need help. We need to help each other. The Church misses this. We have to admit that we do not have it all figured out. This is why at One Generation Away, we have people come and help us distribute food from other churches. Because we need help.

No church can be everything to everyone. No church is equipped to meet every single need, even in one community. The churches that try to be all things to all men never do anything with excellence. These churches end up serving halfheartedly, thinking they are being everything that God wants them to be. In reality, they are not serving with excellence, and they are a fraction of what God wants them to be.

A church needs to know how to serve other churches, but we also need to allow other churches to serve us. We will encourage their gifts by allowing them to serve us. We will promote unity in the body. But it takes admitting that our church does not have all the answers.

I want to be a church that believes in serving churches. We believe in serving our neighborhood. We believe in serving our community. And we teach other people how to serve like we do. This is what the life of the Church should look like. We hold onto nothing, give whatever we have away.

These ideas aren't patented. They're not my ideas. They are God's ideas.

When you truly encounter Jesus in the Church, it is not because He can meet your own needs—He can, but He wants to show you how to meet the needs of others. We have become so self-centered as a society, which has caused churches to become more and more inwardly focused.

I believe in blessing our own people as a church. I love blessing people in my own church. I love going to lunch and fighting over who is going to pay the check. I love trying to out-give people, and trying to bless others in subtle ways. But those things should be the default in the church, and we need to become more intentionally outward-focused.

Acts 4:32-37   Now the multitude of those who believed were of one heart and one soul; neither did anyone say that any of the things he possessed was his own, but they had all things in common. 33 And with great power the apostles gave witness to the resurrection of the Lord Jesus. And great grace was upon them all. 34 Nor was there anyone among them who lacked; for all who were possessors of lands or houses sold them, and brought the proceeds of the things that were sold, 35 and laid them at the apostles' feet; and they distributed to each as anyone had need. 36 And Joses, who was also named Barnabas by the apostles (which is translated Son of Encouragement), a Levite of the country of Cyprus, 37 having land, sold it, and brought the money and laid it at the apostles' feet.

This scripture can be very divisive in our capitalist culture. I think that happens because people preach this passage as if it were some kind of communal hippie movement—one big commune in the book of Acts. I don't think that captures what is at play here.

The times of communes that emerged from the hippie movement failed because they inadvertently encouraged takers and leeches. That is what their flawed design does. People come to a commune because they are lazy, and they want people to do everything for them so they don't have to work—it is human nature. My Bible says if a man doesn't work, don't let him eat.

Jesus was not a slacker. Jesus worked His whole life. He was a carpenter. Carpentry is not a sissy job. It is work—saws, dust, labor, sweat, hammers, nails, blisters, calloused hands.

Don't misunderstand me; we are a serving church. That might sound fun or cute to you. Not all of our food distributions are easy. Once, we had to hike 60 pounds of food to what seemed like the opposite side of Nashville, carrying it through fields, bugs, and heat. There was another distribution we did on May 1, 2010, which locals will remember as a storm that produced 16 inches of rain in two days, flooding all over Nashville. As we were delivering food, it was literally raining sideways. We were serving on Cinco De Mayo one year, standing there with water up to our shins with lightning everywhere while we were setting up tents for the food.

Serving is not for the faint of heart.

The other day I got a phone call; a lady was trying to sell her bakers rack and an armoire on Craigslist. After some time, she finally gave up trying to sell it, and someone gave her my number. She told me, "I just want to donate it and give it to somebody who has need."

That is the Church.

A few days before, my pastor friend Jon Sterns had called and said, "Somebody donated an 18-wheeler to us so we can take supplies down to Alabama for tornado relief." So all of a sudden we have an armoire and bakers rack we can give to someone who has just lost everything.

That is the Church. It may seem small and insignificant to you, but I promise it was not small or insignificant to that family who had lost everything they owned to a tornado.

Wouldn't it be amazing if the Church thought this way all the time? What if our default thought process was, instead of getting 50 bucks on Craigslist for something we're no longer using, to seek out someone in need and make a difference for that person? Maybe then we wouldn't cling so tightly to things; after all, Jesus always chose people over things.

Maybe there is someone in your community who is suffering because of bad decisions. It is not your job to punish that person or teach him or her a lesson. They do not need you to make sure they "get what they deserve." What if the Church was a safe place for that person? What if we showed them grace? What if we simply offered help? Thank God we didn't get what we deserved for our sins.

I think the Church has some work to do when it comes to serving. We have a little skin in the game, but it's time to go all in. And I am preaching to myself, too. Christ's service cost Him everything. We need to be willing to put it all out there.

Elaine and I are close to being empty nesters. What that means for us is that we need to start thinking about how we are going to use our home to serve. That means sacrifice; so I don't see our nest being truly empty any time soon.

I got a call recently from some people that, through a set of circumstances, now need a place to live. We have an opportunity to serve someone, but it is going to cost us. That's when service becomes very real. You start to think, "That sounds great for someone else to do. But that's not my calling." Sorry, that is not under calling; that is under service.

I value my home. I value the privacy and safety that it offers my family. When you have someone live with you, you lose a little bit of that privacy—if you are married, you already know that. Even though you love and cherish your spouse, you have sacrificed the opportunity to shut your door and not think about anyone but yourself for a while. You sacrifice that right in order to love and serve another person. You surrender far more privacy when you invite someone else into your home. But service takes sacrifice.

For the Church to do this well takes discernment. I cannot allow someone to move in forever. There are limits to healthy service. You want to help people; you don't want to enable people. But there has to be a way in which we can help people transition from one place to another.

Instead of sitting around saying, "I'm still just waiting to hear from God," what if we went back and did a checkup? Am I feeding the hungry? Am I bringing the poor to my house? Am I clothing the naked? Am I forgiving people? Am I helping them move forward? If we are not seeing God do the things we believe He should do, what needs to change?

Start to think about what you could do to serve more. *Greater love has no one than this, than to lay down one's life for his friends (John 15:13).* Jesus literally laid down His life and died; but I believe serving is dying to self. That is what it means to lay down your life. You die to self to serve another human being who has nothing to give you in return. That is serving. That is why we need to serve other churches.

I don't have all the answers for what it looks like practically in your community, but it is time to start asking those questions. It is time to realize that your church and the other churches in your community are on the same team; you are fighting the same battle; and you have gifts to offer one another.

Start identifying the needs in your community. That might mean *actually meeting* some of the poorer people in your community. Then you will quickly start to see what their needs are. What if you started finding out their kids' birthdays and offering to throw birthday parties for them, to decorate and make a cake? That costs you very little, but it could be huge for a mom who wants to give that to her child and cannot afford it.

Be creative.

Are they going to start tithing? Probably not. Are they going to attend your church? Maybe, maybe not. But we need to learn to start serving our community with no strings attached. These are your neighbors. They are real people. And God cares deeply for them. It is time for His Church to do the same.

I believe God is calling us to go higher in our service, challenging us to put more skin in the game. You will never out-serve God, because He gave everything. And you won't earn anything, because He has already freely given you life in Christ. This is about the Church being obedient. And I believe that there is blessing in obedience.

SERVING AND YOU

We discussed earlier Ruth's servant's heart and how her service strengthened her relationships with others. But I want to go back to Ruth's story and look at her service in terms of her own situation.

Service is not about what you can get out of it, but I believe that when you serve, you find your truest identity and experience the most blessing.

Ruth 1:1-14 Now it came to pass, in the days when the judges ruled, that there was a famine in the land. And a certain man of Bethlehem, Judah, went to dwell in the country of Moab, he and his wife and his two sons. 2 The name of the man was Elimelech, the name of his wife was Naomi, and the names of his two sons were Mahlon and Chilion—Ephrathites of Bethlehem, Judah. And they went to the country of Moab and remained there.

3 Then Elimelech, Naomi's husband, died; and she was left, and her two sons. 4 Now they took wives of the women of Moab: the name of the one was Orpah, and the name of the other Ruth. And they dwelt there about ten years. 5 Then both Mahlon and Chilion also died; so the woman survived her two sons and her husband.

So here now they have moved to Moab and married two women from Moab. They are not Jewish women. They are not of the Covenant.

6 Then she arose with her daughters-in-law that she might return from the country of Moab, for she had heard in the country of Moab that the Lord had visited His people by giving them bread

So what she is saying is that I want to go back. I want to go back to Judah, to Israel because I hear God is taking care of his children.

7 Therefore she went out from the place where she was, and her two daughters-in-law with her; and they went on the way to return to the land of Judah. 8 And Naomi said to her two daughters-in-law, "Go, return each to her mother's house. The Lord deal kindly with you, as you have dealt with the dead and with me. 9 The Lord grant that you may find rest, each in the house of her husband."

So she kissed them, and they lifted up their voices and wept. 10 And they said to her, "Surely we will return with you to your people."

11 But Naomi said, "Turn back, my daughters; why will you go with me? Are there still sons in my womb, that they may be your husbands? 12 Turn back, my daughters, go— for I am too old to have a husband. If I should say I have hope, if I should have a husband tonight and should also bear sons, 13 would you wait for them till they were grown? Would you restrain yourselves from having husbands? No, my daughters; for it grieves me very much for your sakes that the hand of the Lord has gone out against me!" 14 Then they lifted up their voices and wept again; and Orpah kissed her mother-in-law, but Ruth clung to her.

Naomi recognizes the deep sacrifice it would be for her daughters-in-law to remain with her. She selflessly begs them not to follow her. She wants them to go back to their own lives, instead of carrying the burden of an old widow. But Ruth insists on coming with Naomi. She insists on serving her mother-in-law, and not abandoning her. Ruth is willing to make the sacrifice.

Ruth 1:15-17   And she said, "Look, your sister-in-law has gone back to her people and to her gods; return after your sister-in-law." 16 But Ruth said: "Entreat me not to leave you, Or to turn back from following after you; For wherever you go, I will go; And wherever you lodge, I will lodge; Your people shall be my people, And your God, my God. 17 Where you die, I will die, And there will I be buried. The Lord do so to me, and more also, If anything but death parts you and me."

This is true commitment. We have talked about how service takes commitment. This goes beyond the superficial people-pleasing of our culture. Ruth is not just telling Naomi what she wants to hear. I love the heart of Ruth. She promises, "Naomi, I am going to serve you no matter what the cost, *if anything but death parts you and me.*" Ruth has counted the cost of service.

Ruth 2:1-5   There was a relative of Naomi's husband, a man of great wealth, of the family of Elimelech. His name was Boaz. 2 So Ruth the Moabitess said to Naomi, "Please let me go to the field, and glean heads of grain after him in whose sight I may find favor." And she said to her, "Go, my daughter." 3 Then she left, and went and gleaned in the field after the reapers. And she happened to come to the part of the field belonging to Boaz, who was of the family of Elimelech. 4 Now behold, Boaz came from Bethlehem, and said to the reapers, "The Lord be with you!" And they answered him, "The Lord bless you!" 5 Then Boaz said to his servant who was in charge of the reapers, "Whose young woman is this?"

Ruth's service quickly becomes tangible. It is easy to say, "I promise to stay with you and serve you." Ruth immediately puts her money where her mouth is. She goes to work out in the fields, picking wheat, getting her hands dirty. But this mundane task leads to something extraordinary.

Ruth 2:6-8 So the servant who was in charge of the reapers answered and said, "It is the young Moabite woman who came back with Naomi from the country of Moab. 7 And she said, 'Please let me glean and gather after the reapers among the sheaves.' So she came and has continued from morning until now, though she rested a little in the house."

8 Then Boaz said to Ruth, "You will listen, my daughter, will you not? Do not go to glean in another field, nor go from here, but stay close by my young women."

This is a pivotal turning point. Ruth's obedience to serve gives her a divine connection with Boaz, who notices her and inquires about her. He soon finds out her story—that the reason she is there is to serve her widowed mother-in-law. Boaz recognizes her humility.

Service leads to divine connections. Ruth is not tooting her own horn. She could have easily gone unnoticed. Serving is not meant to draw attention to yourself; it's meant to bless someone else. But if you do that with a right heart, God often will put you in front of the right people in the right place at the right time.

Proverbs 22:29 Do you see a man who excels in his work? he will stand before kings; he will not stand before unknown men.

Now this foreigner, this Moabitess, this poor woman, is about to stand before a great and wealthy man in Israel. Call it luck that Boaz noticed her, but I believe that luck is a byproduct of hard work. Ruth was not trying to be noticed, but her extraordinary humility and determination could not go unnoticed forever.

Ruth 2:9-16 "Let your eyes be on the field which they reap, and go after them. Have I not commanded the young men not to touch you? And when you are thirsty, go to the vessels and drink from what the young men have drawn."

10 So she fell on her face, bowed down to the ground, and said to him, "Why have I found favor in your eyes, that you should take notice of me, since I am a foreigner?"

So she admits she has found favor and says, "I am a foreigner."

11 And Boaz answered and said to her, "It has been fully reported to me, all that you have done for your mother-in-law since the death of your husband, and how you have left your father and your mother and the land of your birth, and have come to a people whom you did not know before. 12 The Lord repay your work, and a full reward be given you by the Lord God of Israel, under whose wings you have come for refuge." 13 Then she said, "Let me find favor in your sight, my lord; for you have comforted me, and have spoken kindly to your maidservant, though I am not like one of your maidservants." 14 Now Boaz said to her at mealtime, "Come here, and eat of the bread, and dip your piece of bread in the vinegar." So she sat beside the reapers, and he passed parched grain to her; and she ate and was satisfied, and kept some back. 15 And when she rose up to glean, Boaz commanded his young men, saying, "Let her glean even among the sheaves, and do not reproach her. 16 Also let grain from the bundles fall purposely for her; leave it that she may glean, and do not rebuke her."

Ruth's desperate need for food is apparent, because she holds some back. Boaz notices. But she has so much favor with him that he instructs his workers to allow her to take extra. When you serve faithfully, God will provide.

You don't have to wait for circumstances to be perfect in your life to serve others. Ruth's identity has been torn away from her. Not only is she a widow, but her sister and mother-in-law have lost their husbands as well. This is a dark time for Ruth and her family. Yet she still decides to serve.

Elaine and I have seen over and over that in the midst of our greatest trials we simply needed to go serve someone else. Even in the midst of our darkest moments, we can still serve.

You don't have to be part of the "in crowd" to serve. Ruth admits she is a foreigner; she knows she's not in the "in crowd." But Boaz recognizes her humility, and he invites her in. He gives her a new identity: "You are covered under the wings of the Lord God Almighty."

Service gives us identity.

Perhaps the biggest crisis we have in the Church today is an identity crisis. We have forgotten who we are in Christ and who Christ is in us.

John 14:7 If you had known Me, you would have known My Father also; and from now on you know Him and have seen Him.